KU-309-302

KC
9b5
.A5
.MCI

Social Science Library
Oxford University Library Services
Manor Road
Oxford OX1 3UQ

WITHDRAWN

Zimbabwe
The Struggle for Health

A community approach for farmworkers

Chris McIvor

Catholic Institute for International Relations

First published 1995
Catholic Institute for International Relations (CIIR)
Unit 3, Canonbury Yard, 190a New North Road, London N1 7BJ, UK

Zimbabwe: The Struggle for Health – A community approach for farmworkers © CIIR 1995
All rights reserved

British Library Cataloguing in Publication Data
A catalogue record for this book is available from the British Library

ISBN 1 85287 122 9

Cover and text photographs: Chris McIvor
Cover and text design: Jan Brown Designs
Printed by the Russell Press, Nottingham, UK

Part of the International Cooperation for Development's *Development in Action* series.

Contents

INTERNATIONAL
COOPERATION
FOR DEVEL●PMENT

International Cooperation for Development (ICD) sends skilled people to work with local groups in the Third World.

By sharing skills with people and communities in the Third World, ICD development workers contribute to these communities challenging poverty, achieving self-reliance and lasting development.

ICD development workers are active in many fields, from midwives to doctors, agronomists to nutritionists, water engineers to mechanics, administration trainers to finance advisors.

ICD works in the Dominican Republic, Ecuador, El Salvador, Honduras, Haiti, Namibia, Nicaragua, Peru, Somaliland/Somalia, Yemen and Zimbabwe.

ICD is the technical cooperation department of CIIR. Founded in 1940 to encourage people to work for a free and democratic Europe, CIIR's work for social justice now extends across four continents.

This book forms part of CIIR's and ICD's **Development in Action** series. Other publications in this series include:

Zimbabwe Steps Ahead: Community rehabilitation and people with disabilities
(96pp, illustrated, 1990, £4.50)
Based upon interviews with disabled people, their families and rehabilitation workers, this book describes Zimbabwe's unique programme of community based rehabilitation and the belief that people with disabilities can become valued and fully participating members of society.

Nicaragua Testing the Water: From village wells to national plan
(60pp, illustrated, 1989, £3.50)
Safe water saves lives. Set against Nicaragua's struggle for health, this book describes a pioneering project that became a national plan. It is a development success story based on a crucial concept: the active and informed support of local people.

For further information contact:
CIIR, Unit 3, Canonbury Yard, 190a New North Road, London N1 7BJ.

Facing page: A woman on a commercial farm near Mvurwi, northern Zimbabwe, and the hut where she now lives with her grandchildren.

Acknowledgements

My acknowledgements go to all those who contributed to the realisation of this book. In particular I would like to thank Josephine Mutandiro of SCF (UK) whose assistance was invaluable in providing me with the contacts among farmworkers, farm-owners, trade unionists, health workers and rural council officials from whom I obtained a greater understanding of the experience of farm labour in Zimbabwe. Many individual and group interviews were conducted during our visits to commercial farms and the fact that all contributors are not named individually does not detract from the debt I owe them. I would also like to thank Rene Loewenson, Carol Thompson and Lloyd Sachikonye for their invaluable comments. My final thanks go to ICD with whom I worked for seven years in Zimbabwe and who supported the research and publication of this book.

Chris McIvor
January 1995

Glossary and list of abbreviations and acronyms

African reserves areas onto which people were forcibly moved, usually to remove them from high quality agricultural land (former name for tribal trust lands)
AFC Agricultural Finance Corporation
BSAC British South Africa Company
CFU Commercial Farmers Union
chibaro system of forced labour established by the Portuguese in 1899
chimurenga popular name for the war of 1896-7 in which the Shona and Ndebele peoples fought together against the British
communal lands tribal trust lands as renamed in 1980
FHW farm health worker
GAPWUZ The General Agricultural and Plantation Workers Union of Zimbabwe
ICD International Cooperation for Development
mugwazo piecework task
n'angas traditional healers
LSF large-scale commercial farm
NGO non-government organisation
PHC primary health care
PMD Provincial Medical Director
RALSC Rhodesian Africal [or Native] Labour Supply Commission
SCF The Save the Children Fund
SIDA Swedish International Development Authority
TBA traditional birth attendant
tribal trust lands (TTLs) former name for communal lands
VHW village health worker
ZANU(PF) Zimbabwe African National Union (Patriotic Front)
ZINATHA Zimbabwe National Traditional Healers Association

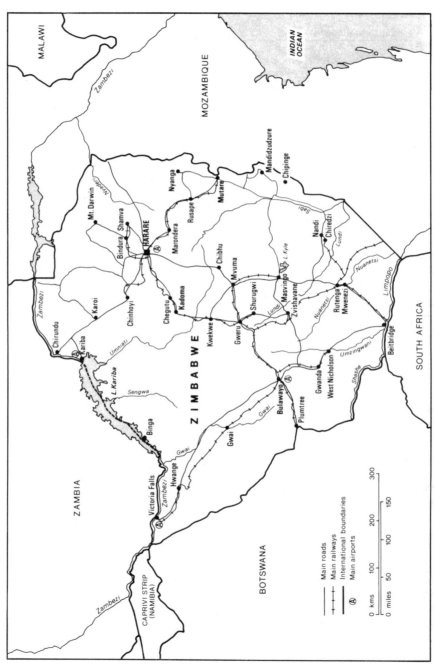

Source: Country Profile on Zimbabwe. Reproduced with the permission of the Economist Intelligence Unit.

Introduction

The journey by road from Harare to Centenary in the north of Zimbabwe takes only two hours yet within that time one could be forgiven for thinking that one had passed through two very distinct and different countries. The road services the agricultural heartland of Mashonaland Central province, the country's main exporter of tobacco and horticultural products and a significant contributor of maize, cotton and citrus. Neat rows of crops and trees stretch to the horizon. Fat, well-fed cattle graze in irrigated fields. The economic development of the area is evident in the well-maintained roads that pass through it, the electrified tobacco-curing barns and grain storage facilities every few miles, the large, stately homes and manicured lawns of the farm owners who enjoy most of its wealth.

Yet every so often away from the road, but not quite out of sight, another spectacle intrudes upon this idyll. These are the compounds of the thousands of workers that have made this wealth possible. Flimsy huts of mud and thatch are huddled together with little evidence of the electricity, water and tarred roads that serve the houses of the owners and managers. Thin children dressed in rags contrast with the well-fed cattle in neighbouring fields. Occasionally a few smarter, more solid dwellings are lined up along the side of the road in open view of the passing traveller. These are the houses of a small, select section of the labour force, the permanent workers whose conditions farm owners can display when they point to the improvements that have taken place in recent years. But almost invariably behind these are the squalid huts and meagre facilities of the majority, the evidence of poverty that is the reverse side of the agricultural success story of the province.

There are approximately 4,500 large-scale commercial farms (LSFs) in Zimbabwe, the vast majority of which are owned by white farmers or multinational corporations. In units covering areas from 2,000 to over 100,000 acres they occupy some 40 per cent of the total land surface of the country and produce most of its agricultural wealth through exports of tobacco, tea, coffee, sugar, cotton and horticultural products. A 1985 survey published by the Central Statistics Office indicated that 51 per cent of LSF acreage is located on rich,

A woman on a commercial farm near Mvurwi, northern Zimbabwe, and the hut where she now lives with her grandchildren.

arable soils of provinces like Mashonaland Central where high rainfall, good communications and easy market access have favoured productivity. Those private estates located in the less fertile regions of southern Zimbabwe make up for the poverty of soil and rainfall by the extent of their property. Cattle ranches, some of which are in excess of 100,000 acres, take up most of the land in the southern provinces of Matabeleland and Masvingo.

International involvement in the LSF sector has increased since the 1950s when multinational companies began to expand their operations in then Rhodesia. By 1980 while local farmers constituted 70 per cent of LSF landowners, they owned only 23 per cent of cultivated land. Foreign-owned companies and in particular multinationals mainly based in the UK, South Africa and USA (such as Lonrho, Anglo-American, Thomas Meikle Trust) who owned the rest, accounted for 75 per cent of gross profits in the agricultural sector (see Riddell 1980, p19). Since the 1970s production trends also began to change with an increasing use of machinery and chemicals to increase crop yields and a diversification to agricultural commodities with a more favourable international market. Thus cotton, winter-irrigated cereals, soya beans, sugar and tea expanded while food-crop production declined. This diversification increased international linkages such as inputs of pesticides, fertilisers, improved seed varieties and mechanical equipment. Dependance on foreign markets for exports and foreign companies for imports to sustain the industry has meant that the LSF sector can count on a considerable international lobby to pressurise the government in its favour.

Cautioning governments in Africa not to threaten the position of commercial farmers, a World Bank report in 1983 outlined its preferences for the continent:

Priority to smallholders does not mean that only they warrant attention. The agricultural sector is highly dualistic in some countries, with large private farms providing major shares of marketed output. Any growth oriented strategies must include these islands of high productivity agriculture.

(World Bank 1983, p53)

Yet for all agriculture's much-vaunted economic success and contribution to exports, surveys before and after Zimbabwean independence in 1980 have consistently shown that the labour force which ensured this productivity has not shared in its benefits.[1] A male farm labourer in 1977 could expect to live 16 years less than his Rhodesian employer. His children under five years old were more prone to severe malnutrition and stunting than in any other sector of the economy. His family were more likely to live in a mud and thatch dwelling with less access to clean water and sanitation than his neighbours in the peasant farming areas. And his children were less likely to attend school since the number of educational facilities in commercial farms lagged way behind those in the rest of the country. Although exact numbers are hard to establish due to the seasonality and mobility of much of the labour on commercial farms, recent estimates put the total number of people living in LSF areas at some 3 million, roughly 20–25 per cent of the total population of the country (Loewenson 1992, p*viii*).

Faced with the entrenchment of the LSF farmer in the political and economic system of Zimbabwe, checked by an international lobby that has insisted on the sanctity of private property, confronted by a multiplicity of social and economic needs among many sections of the population after 1980, the government of Zimbabwe has been unable to achieve the significant improvements for farm labour that it announced as part of its intention at independence. Yet one service which has provided a forum for encouraging some change in their conditions is its primary health care programme. The Farm Health Worker (FHW) scheme arose out of the Ministry of Health's 'Health For All' action plan, which, after independence in 1980, aimed to decentralise health care and promotion to the rural people who had been most ignored during the colonial era. While initially targeted on the communal lands, those areas of the country to which the indigenous population were forcibly removed during colonial times to make way for commercial farms, an FHW scheme did arise as an offshoot of this

---

1 See:
   a. Clarke, DG, 1977. *Agricultural and plantation workers in Rhodesia*, Mambo Press, Harare.
   b. United Nations, 1977, *United Nations demographic year book*, Harare, p396.
   c. Chikanza, I, Paxton, D, Loewenson, R and Laing, R, 1981. 'The health status of farmworker communities in Zimbabwe', *The Central African Journal of Medicine* (May).

development.

Although instigated by the Ministry of Health in a pilot programme in Mashonaland Central province in the early 1980s, it also opened the door for several other Ministries as well as international non-government organisations (NGOs) to play a part in addressing some of the problems associated with farm labour. Organisations such as International Cooperation for Development (ICD) were asked to support initiatives in this area through the provision of technical expertise, doctors and therapists, that the ministry needed at this time. Others such as Save the Children Fund (UK) provided financial assistance and programme support for the development and extension of the programme beyond its initial pilot phase.

The sheer scale of the problems confronting farm labour and the scarcity of national resources to solve it has also meant that agencies and ministries could have no significant impact without the particpation and cooperation of the community itself. In other words they have had to listen, and only those health workers, programme officers and ministry personnel who have listened carefully to the needs, wishes and priorities of the people they are seeking to help have achieved the kind of success that gives hope for the future.

While conditions for the majority of workers and their families continue to be poor and while the structures that have created such impoverishment remain intact, this book claims that there is enough evidence of change to merit some optimism. These changes have largely to do with farmworkers' perception of their own situation and their attempts, however slow due to the difficulties they face, to alter this. One farm health worker from Mashonaland Central province put it in these words:

We have come to see that health is not only something that we receive but something we must do. It is more than a matter of drugs and doctors. It is a question of changing our own and others' attitudes, our own conditions, doing things for ourselves and our families.

The first chapter of this book describes the origin and growth of the commercial farming sector in Zimbabwe. The second details the social conditions of farm labour which the government inherited at independence. Chapter 3 discusses the impediments to change in the period thereafter and the ways in which farm owners have managed to bypass some of the legislation that was brought in to protect workers. Chapter 4 describes the Farm Health Worker scheme, its origin, development and support from other organisations. Chapter 5 discusses the programme's specific implementation on a farm in Mashonaland Central province. Chapter 6 deals with the problems that continue to confront its development. The final chapter concludes with a series of recommendations to enhance the success and expansion of the programme.

1
Control and dispossession

The lure of gold

When the 196 men of the 'pioneer column' crossed from South Africa into what was later to become Southern Rhodesia on 11 July 1890, they expected to find a fabulous land of wealth and riches. For several decades travellers and explorers had brought back stories of abundant gold to be found north of the Limpopo river in the kingdom of the Mashonas. The English explorer Frederick Selous related that as far back as the fifteenth century Arab traders along the coasts of southeast Africa had spoken of extensive gold mining in the interior:

> *These gold mines were being worked by the natives of the country, who used the gold as a medium of exchange to buy the goods brought to them by the Arabs, and for centuries before this time their ancestors had, in all probability, made use of gold whose value had been taught them by the ancient builders of the temple of Zimbabwe.*
> (Selous 1893, p335)

The lure of the yellow metal, given impetus by the discovery of the goldfields around Johannesburg in the 1880s, turned the attention of entrepreneurs and prospectors further north in the hope that the vast fortunes realised in the Transvaal could be replicated in Zimbabwe.

The pioneer column was funded by Cecil John Rhodes, a wealthy British politician and businessman who had established his fortune in South Africa with the discovery of diamonds in the 1870s. On the pretext that colonial intervention was necessary in Mashonaland to protect the indigenous Shona people against the fierce and intrepid Ndebele, a branch of the Zulus who had entered the region several decades previously, Rhodes negotiated with the British government for a Royal Charter for the British South Africa Company (BSAC) which he established in 1889. This charter gave him the right to occupy and exploit the land and mineral resources, including the gold deposits reputed to be in abundance throughout the area.

With the promise of mining concessions and guarantees of land the 196 volunteers he recruited and supplied penetrated to the heart of Mashonaland and on 12 September 1890, raised the British flag at what was to be named Fort Salisbury, after the prime minister of the time. Five years later the kingdom of Mashonaland was given the name Rhodesia. The men of the pioneer column were soon joined by a wave of prospectors, administrators and adventurers from further south. In 1894 the European presence in Mashonaland had risen to over 5,000. For the indigenous population, claims by these newcomers that they were there to protect them against the depredations of the Ndebele must have seemed a bitter mockery. By this time the BSAC had constituted itself into a de facto government establishing an administrative and legal infrastructure to run the country. Much of the finances for this were raised by imposition of taxes on local people and the confiscation of their land and possessions if they refused to pay. The tax was collected in Matabeleland (the southern part of the country) in 1894 through the confiscation of 80 per cent of the people's cattle, their traditional form of wealth and security. By 1895 in some districts of Mashonaland as much as one third of the cattle, sheep and goats were taken by force because of the unwillingness or inability of the local population to pay a newly introduced hut tax (Schmidt 1992, p38).

Six years after the invasion of their country both the Shona and Ndebele rose in revolt, much to the surprise of the British who preferred to believe that both groups would never unite in opposition to them. Hostilities continued for over a year and it was only with the arrest and subsequent hanging of the leaders of the rebellion that the conflict finally ended.

This war, however, which was popularly known as 'chimurenga' was to inspire a later generation of Zimbabweans to fight for majority rule and independence. From the first arrival of Rhodes' pioneers in 1890 to the establishment of democratic government in 1980 the reasons for conflict between the indigenous population and settlers remained the same, the control of land and its wealth. One old man born in 1902 explained:

The whites did not take our country in a ceremonious way. They were feasting on our forefathers' blood. The only way we could get it back was through waging a war against them.

(Zengene quoted in Jensen 1992, p30)

Commercial farms and dispossession

Despite the establishment of numerous mines in the 1890s and early part of the twentieth century the fabled gold and precious stones did not materialise to the extent that was hoped for. Gold-bearing strata were thin and found deep underground, demanding extensive time and labour to mine. When the directors

The communal lands are situated in the poorest agricultural regions of the country. Pressure on resources has fuelled popular demands for change in the land ownership pattern, where 4,500 commercial farmers own some 45 per cent of the total land area and some 6-7 million peasants occupy the rest. Here communal farmers plough land in communal areas in preparation for planting.

of the British South Africa Company toured the colony in 1907 they found that it was virtually bankrupt. Yet what the country lacked in precious minerals it made up for in the vast tracts of rich, arable land found in many parts of the country, especially in the north and east. Shortly after their visit, the BSAC was to adopt a policy to diversify away from mining and to encourage the development of the commercial farming sector.

To attract settler farmers the state offered free agricultural training and a variety of services. In 1912 a land bank was established to provide European farmers with loans for the purchase of farms, livestock and agricultural equipment as well as to finance improvements in irrigation and fencing. Fertilisers, seeds and stocks were made available at subsidised prices. Roads and other facilities were constructed close to European settlements. The success of these incentives can be seen in the rate of increase in the number of European farms between 1904 and 1914. By the latter date there were 2,040 European-occupied farms covering 183,400 acres compared to the 20,000 acres worked by 545 settlers a decade earlier (Schmidt 1992, p66).

In order to ensure that European commercial farms remained well ahead of local peasant production, the BSAC and subsequent governments in Rhodesia pursued a policy of discrimination against the indigenous population. Their first strategy was to appropriate the best agricultural land for the establishment of European farms. This policy was enshrined in law in 1920 with the adoption of the recommendations of a Native Reserves Commission. African farming areas were to be reduced by one million acres of the most fertile, well-watered land close to markets and communication routes. The population in these areas was to be forcibly evicted and removed to what were called African Reserves and later tribal trust lands (TTLs). After independence these areas were renamed communal lands.

Tribal trust lands were sited on arid, impoverished soils. Tsetse fly was also prevalent causing sleeping sickness in humans and a disease called nagana in cattle which decimated the herds of African farmers. A further encumbrance was the prohibition on hunting wild game, a traditional source of food for the local population during times of hardship. In 1923 wild animals were categorised as 'royal game' belonging to the state. The indigenous people effectively suffered a double expropriation, denied both the better land suitable for agriculture and the wildlife which could survive in the marginal areas to which they had been removed.

Evictions were carried out without any warnings or consultation with the people who had occupied these areas for centuries. One peasant farmer recalls the removal of his family from a fertile area in northern Zimbabwe:

> *We were made to move from our area by a European who had bought the land. 'Do you know an area called Marirangwe?', he asked us. We knew the area, and then he said, 'Now is the time for threshing. That's what you must do and then you must leave this area and go to Marirangwe. This land is now mine'. Then he took some cloth and hoisted it as a flag. We told the elders of our clan that they would have to go to Hartley and report that a mad European had come to our area. When they came to Hartley, they were told that it was Mr. Hallas, and that they should hurry up, take all their things with them, or else our property would be burnt.*
>
> (Quoted in Jensen 1992, p79)

The second strategy to minimise African competition was to enact a series of laws which limited their access to local and international markets. Indigenous farmers in the earlier part of the century had proved themselves highly competent in diversifying their production to cater for the expanded food needs of mining compounds and newly established urban areas. As the number of white settlers increased they began to press for protective legislation to guarantee this opportunity for themselves. In 1931 a Maize Control Act was passed which established a state-run board to parcel out shares of the domestic and international market to African and European producers. Mainly skewed in favour of the latter, African farmers were also forced to sell their maize through European traders who demanded a large commission for this service. By 1934 white commercial farmers received on average a price three to four times higher for a bag of maize than did their African counterparts (Schmidt 1992, p76).

Further legislation also adversely affected African sales of cattle. Dipping fees were raised as well as a substantial levy on sales of animals for slaughter in peasant areas. The Natives Registration Act of 1936 prevented Africans from selling their produce in European areas of Salisbury and other urban centres, a prohibition which did not extend to white traders in African suburbs. While the sale of curios, baskets and other crafts was permitted, vegetables, chickens, eggs, butter and other foodstuffs could be sold only by Africans in African locations.

Cheap labour for commercial farms

Land appropriation continued over subsequent decades as the state continued to pursue a policy of attracting European settlers to the colony. Southern Rhodesia became a magnet for poor, unskilled and semi-skilled whites mainly from Britain, with some from South Africa, whose aspirations to wealth and status were realised at the expense of the indigenous population. By the early 1970s, when the number of immigrants began to decline in the wake of civil conflict, over 260,000 Europeans, out of a total population of some 8 million, were resident in the country.

The establishment of white commercial farms continued unabated. In 1951 a Land Husbandry Act prohibited African farmers from owning more than six acres of land at a time when white farmers held a minimum plot of 750 acres. Of a total of around 6,000 European farms, 895 were in excess of 10,000 acres at that time (Loewenson 1992, p38). In 1962 a further four million hectares of African land were seized by the state for redistribution to white farmers. In 1969 the Land Tenure Act formalised the racial segregation of land by prohibiting blacks from purchasing farms or property outside their reserves. Humphrey Wightwick, a parliamentarian in the 1960s, was quite blatant about the system that openly discriminated in favour of the European farmer:

> *To the south of us we have a country which practices a thing called apartheid. Here in Southern Rhodesia we do not speak Afrikaans, so we pronounce it the Land Apportionment Act.*

> (Quoted in Rifkind 1968, p212)

The seizure of fertile land and the exclusion of African farmers from markets for their produce were not solely designed to minimise local competition against European farmers. Another principal aim of these policies was to create a class of wage labourers, a reservoir of young men available to private enterprise at the cheapest possible price.[1] The creation of a labour reserve was originally intended for the mining enterprises established in the early part of the colonial period. But as more land was opened up for commercial agriculture the demand for workers prompted European farmers to pressurise the government to speed up the process. The hut and poll taxes, the cattle levies, and the dog licence fees imposed on the indigenous population not only helped fuel the administrative wheels of the colonial state but were also designed to force African peasants on to the labour market to enable them to pay these duties.

Most households initially resisted working in the harsh conditions of the mines and commercial farms. A Native Commissioner of Goromonzi district in central Zimbabwe acknowledged in the 1930s that the wages given to farm workers of 15 shillings per month would not pay for the clothing of their wives and children let alone any of their own requirements (Schmidt 1992, p74). At the same time, resentment felt by the people against seizure of land which had once been theirs fuelled resistance to contributing to the wealth of those who had taken it by force.

During the initial few decades of colonial rule the indigenous population were largely able to avoid wage labour by expanding their agricultural production to a level where taxes could be paid. But by the 1930s the tribal trust lands were unable to support the growing number of Africans who had been relocated to them.

Rhodesia was classified into five main agricultural zones, or 'natural regions', which indicated the agricultural potential of each region (Roussos 1988, p56):

1 Specialised and diversified farming region: with a rainfall of over 1,000mm/year, this area is particularly suitable for forestry, fruit and intensive livestock production.
2 Intensive farming region: slightly lower rainfalls of 750–1,000mm/year make this region suitable for intensive crop and/or livestock production.
3 Semi-intensive farming region: this zone has 650–800mm rainfall/year which comes in infrequent heavy falls. There are fairly severe mid-season dry spells, making this region marginal as far as maize, tobacco and cotton are concerned.
4 Semi-extensive farming region: rainfall in this region drops to 450–650mm/year. Thus the land is mainly suitable for livestock production.
5 Extensive farming region: the low erratic rainfall in this area means that this land is only suitable for extensive cattle and game ranching.

Most of the tribal trust lands were situated in agricultural regions 3 to 5, those parts of the country with low rainfall, poor soils and unsuitable for intensive crop

---

1 Claimed Cecil Rhodes in 1894: 'It must be brought home to them that in the future nine-tenths of them will have to spend their own lives in daily labour, in physical work, in manual labour.' (Quoted in Davies 1990, p1.)

production or large numbers of livestock. The more fertile areas, classified as regions 1 and 2 had largely become the exclusive property of the commercial farming sector. Increasing population pressure, soil erosion, periodic drought and geographical distance from markets created a situation where the population within the African reserves could no longer resist the pressure to sell their labour to the highest bidder. While an estimated 20 per cent of indigenous men were employed in wage labour between 1911 and 1922, about 50 per cent had moved into this sector by 1932. Wage earnings around this time had also overtaken revenues from agricultural production as the principal source of income among peasant households (Schmidt 1992, p73).

One labourer on a commercial farm in Centenary district, northern Zimbabwe, relates the factors that prompted his family to abandon their plot in the tribal trust lands in the 1950s:

My parents worked hard to make some kind of living on the bit of land we were allocated by the chief in our area. But things got worse from year to year. The soil was poor. The rainfall was bad. Though we had no desire to work for the Europeans it was either that or starvation.

Migrant labour

Nevertheless the reluctance of the indigenous population to enter a system which they knew was exploitative forced commercial farmers to explore possibilities of acquiring cheap labour further afield. The main recruiting grounds were Nyasaland (now Malawi), Northern Rhodesia (now Zambia) and Mozambique which were to provide substantial numbers of workers for the cotton, tobacco and tea plantations of northern and eastern Zimbabwe. Importation of extra-territorial labour was already taking place as far back as the early 1900s when farmers and mine owners jointly established a collective recruitment agency. This was later developed into the Rhodesian Native Labour Supply Commission (RNLSC), which was established as a parastatal after the Second World War when tobacco farmers could not supply their labour demands from inside the country. Under the contract system the RNLSC imported an average of 14,000 workers per year from 1946 to 1971. By 1966, 54 per cent of male labour in the commercial farming sector came from the surrounding countries (Duncan 1973, p73).

The factors that prompted people from these territories to accept work in southern Rhodesia were largely the same as those which were forcing local peasants to enter the labour system. Dispossession and the collapse of local agriculture under colonialism afflicted all the indigenous inhabitants of the region. But in a country like Mozambique conditions were so appalling that work in a neighbouring colony was regarded as an opportunity. Because there were not enough settlers to take over the land the Portuguese had established a system of

Jonathan Kadandara came from Malawi in the 1950s to work on the commercial farms of northern Zimbabwe. Without savings of any kind he now survives through the charity of his neighbours.

forced labour called *chibaro* in 1899, a practice which continued until 1961. This stated that all native inhabitants of the Portuguese provinces were subject to a legal obligation to work on private estates. If they did not comply the public authorities could force them to do so.[2]

Brutalised by police and other military authorities, chibaro labourers were not entitled to food or lodging, were often beaten, and received little or no wages. Although women were supposedly exempt they were often forced to work and were abused by overseers and farm owners. The legal time limit of six months was often ignored and some men found themselves shipped to distant plantations for as long as two years. Jonas Sengado who lives on a commercial farm in northern Zimbabwe recalls the reasons that prompted him to flee Mozambique in 1939 with his brother:

> *Conditions under the Portuguese were terrible. We were forced to work on cotton plantations for nothing. They beat us. They took our women. It was our dream to escape. People talked of Salisbury as a better place so like many others we abandoned our homes and left.*

---

2   For a discussion of 'chibaro' in Mozambique, see Thompson (1991), pp13–15.

For Jonathan Kadandara from Malawi, poverty in his own country forced him to look for work elsewhere. He remembers the time when a white farmer from Rhodesia arrived in his village and called for workers. In return for their labour he promised to provide them with accommodation, food, other allowances and wages which would be sent back to their own villages to support the families they would leave behind. Jonathan left his village in the 1950s to work on that farm. Ten years later he returned home only to find that no allowances had been returned to his village. Economic desperation forced him to return south again in the hope that one day he would have enough saved to return to Malawi with money and possessions to establish himself in his community. Now that Jonathan is old and without savings of any kind, that dream has dwindled over the years into nothing:

I don't think about going back any longer. There is no point in hoping for something that will never happen.

2

The social conditions of labour

Minimising the social costs of production

One of the promises given by the Rhodesian government to prospective settlers from Europe wishing to farm land was a ready supply of cheap labour. This was to form a major part of the comparative advantage these farmers were to enjoy over their agricultural rivals from other countries. Cash-crop production faced several obstacles. The country lacked access to the sea, and transport costs through South African and Mozambican ports reduced its margin of profitability from exports. The relatively late development of colonialism also meant that Rhodesia initially lacked the established infrastructure and markets developed by other producers. The large-scale seizure of rich, arable land and the exploitation of indigenous labour were intended to balance out these disadvantages. The system worked so well that in the 1930s Rhodesian businesses were said to be enjoying 'the cheapest Black labour in the British Empire'.[1]

In order to maximise their profits, commercial farmers kept the social costs of production to a minimum. Wages, housing, health care and social amenities were regarded as unfortunate financial burdens. One justification for this low level of expenditure was the claim by farmers and government officials that the single male migrant worker from the reserves would be supported by the family he had left behind. But having lost the labour of their husbands, fathers and brothers the burden on women became excessive. The bulk of agricultural production in these areas increasingly rested on their shoulders – estimated by one commission in 1944 at 80 per cent[2] – as well as the care of the sick, disabled and retired workers dismissed from commercial farms when they were no longer productive. A Native Commissioner of Mutare, eastern Zimbabwe in 1930 explained the role of women and children in the labour system:

---

1   See Phimister, IR, 1983. 'Zimbabwe: the path of capitalist development' in *History of Central Africa*, Longmans, London, 2nd volume, p280.
2   'Native production and trade commission', p7 Jesuit Archives, Southern Rhodesia, cited in Schmidt 1992.

As a rule the head of the family goes to work to earn his tax and money for some requirements. Meanwhile his wife remains at the kraal (homestead) to grow food for the whole family. Only a very small proportion of natives in employment earn enough to purchase food for their families.

(Quoted in Schmidt 1992, p82)

As taxes became more punitive, and some African reserves were unable to support the increasing numbers of people crowded upon them, peasant households were forced to enter the wage labour system. This included women and children whom farmers came to see as a ready source of exploitable labour. Increasingly from the 1920s onwards the fields of commercial farmers were ploughed, weeded and harvested by entire families. Given the level of economic desperation owners could dictate conditions of employment. Women were paid consistently less than men and often received payment in kind such as maize meal during times of drought, supplies of sugar and tea from the farmers' store (at marked up prices) or very often nothing but the payment of debt their husbands had incurred as credit to the farmer.[3]

One labour practice that developed was the piece task or *mugwazo*. This was a task set by the farmer for a worker to complete by a certain time. Often unable to finish such a duty on his own, his wife and children were forced to help him without extra remuneration of any kind.

Workers received no protection from the state against the practices of unscrupulous employers. Wages were used to regulate profits. During the international economic slump of the 1930s many farmers suspended salaries altogether and simply granted food as payment for labour. At the same time there was no obligation enforced on farm owners to provide any facilities to the large communities increasingly being established on their properties. Indeed some farmers saw the provision of services such as health care and education as spoiling the natives, making them accustomed to rights and privileges that would compromise their willingness to work.[4]

John Mushore was an agricultural demonstrator employed by the government during the 1940s and 1950s to instruct workers on commercial farms on the

---

3 When Lawrence Vambe visited relatives in a reserve in 1927, he found that men, women and children were working in the fields of neighbouring European settlers: 'We did not get any food during the day. Working in boiling sun and on only one meal which we had at home, we had to get rid of the quantities of weeds, which grew in profusion between the maize plants. We were not expected to take rest breaks and if we did and were noticed by the farmer, that meant less maize meal at the end of the day.' Vambe, L, 1976. *From Rhodesia to Zimbabwe*, Heinemann, London, pp22–23.

4 Early missionaries seemed to share this view, 'The native being by nature indolent and easy going,' asserted one Jesuit, 'one of the most important points in his education is to accustom him to habits of industry and make him sensible of the folly and danger of idling away his time'. Another concluded that it was not the Jesuits' attempt to promote a form of education that would 'result in contempt of the pick and shovel' (quoted in Schmidt 1992, p127).

principles of soil conservation. He recalls his meeting with a white farmer near Gweru in the Midlands province of central Zimbabwe:

> *When I came the white man took me to his hall and said to me – 'Here you are on the land of clever people, we do not want to hear anyone talking about schools, we do not want to hear anyone talking about Sundays. If we hear anyone talking about that, we know that you are the one who will have told them. Your role here is only to teach them how to prevent soil erosion on the farm. That's all.'*
>
> (Quoted in Jensen 1992, p53)

A number of key laws and prohibitions were introduced by the state during the colonial period to control the flow of labour and restrict unionisation and political activity among African farmworkers. These included the following:

- The Master and Servant Act (1899)
- The Pass Law (1901)
- The Private Locations Ordinance (1910)
- The Industrial Conciliation Act (1934)
- The Native Registration Act (1936)
- The Sedition Act (1936)
- The Compulsory Native Labour Act (1943)
- The Foreign Migratory Act (1958)

The most notorious of these was the first, the Master and Servant Act of 1899, described by one commentator as 'an infamous charter of serfdom' (Loewenson and Chinhori 1986, p26). Under this Act workers were effectively made the property of the employer. They required permission to live with their families and could not refuse to accompany their 'master on any journey within Southern Rhodesia'. No leave provisions were prescribed nor obligations on the employer to provide housing or sickness benefits. The Act indicated punishments for a range of offences such as absenteeism at work, desertion, careless performance, refusal to obey an employer, abusiveness and making use of employers' property. In 1978 it was documented that approximately two African workers were being prosecuted under the Act every working day of the year.[5]

Amai Raymond recalls the past

Although there was a lack of statistics on social conditions of labour before 1980 those that did exist indicated the scale of the problem right up until

---

5   See International Labour Organisation, 1978. *Labour Conditions and Discrimination in Southern Rhodesia*, ILO, Geneva.

A tractor ploughs land on a commercial estate in Mashonaland West province.

independence. With regard to health status, studies published in the 1970s reported undernutrition to be a severe problem among farmworker communities. At a mission hospital in Chimora tribal trust land, 75 per cent of tuberculosis patients were found to have come from neighbouring commercial farms in 1976. The same report found that farmworkers were housed in cramped compounds which 'are the most densely populated settlements to be found in Rhodesia today'. School enrolment figures were the lowest in the country.[6]

Amai Raymond's story is typical of many descriptions given by farm workers that this author interviewed. Although some of the conditions she describes have changed in the interim due to a more sympathetic owner, the picture of the past she presents is not a distant one. Born in the communal lands of Mashonaland Central province, poverty forced Amai Raymond's family to look for employment in the commercial farms nearby. She recalls the conditions that greeted them when they arrived at Tsoro farm near Centenary over 30 years ago. The farm covered several thousand hectares of prime agricultural land and, like most estates in the province, had concentrated on tobacco production which had experienced a major boom in the post-war years. Tobacco was a labour-intensive product and one in three farmworkers in the country at that time were employed in tobacco farming.

Some 600 labourers and their families worked on Tsoro farm in those days, although seasonal employment would swell the numbers considerably during the peak planting, weeding and harvesting seasons. The workers lived in three

---

6   Statistics from Clarke op cit (note 1, Introduction), pp21–34.

Tobacco is Zimbabwe's main agricultural export and a labour-intensive crop: it is estimated that one in three jobs in the agricultural sector are related to its production. Inhalation of tobacco dust among farm workers can cause health problems. Young children are particularly at risk, brought into the tobacco barns by their mothers who often lack access to childcare when they are working.

settlements located in different parts of the property. These were nothing more than random collections of huts erected by the workers themselves after they were offered employment by the farmer. 'There was no such thing as a village or community,' Amai Raymond recalls. 'We had temporary shelters without amenities of any kind.'

All of the houses were made of mud and thatch. Due to uncertainty of employment and the lack of protection against dismissal, families were reluctant to improve their accommodation substantially. During the rainy season the more flimsy shelters were washed away. There were no taps in any of the compounds, nor a nearby borehole to collect water. Everyone drew their supply from the dam a few kilometres away, which they shared with the farmer's cattle. Latrines were a luxury that only came later. 'Before then we used the open country'.

There was little or no access to childcare facilities. Since many of the mothers were obliged to work this left younger children unattended.

Even the older, more responsible children had to work in the fields. There was no one to look after the younger ones. Accidents were common. They were always ill. Although harvest time was when we got most money it was also when the health of our families suffered most.

The heavy workload of mothers during periods of peak labour adversely affected the family in other ways. Domestic duties such as childcare, household cleanliness, food preparation and vegetable production were neglected.

The health of the farm labourers at Tsoro was poor, Amai Raymond claims. Many of her own brothers and sisters did not survive beyond infancy. The nearest health centre to the farm was too far to walk and access to a doctor depended on the goodwill of the farmer. In the absence of professional advice and other medical resources there was a heavy dependence during those years on self-help remedies, traditional healers and the goodwill of the farmer's wife who occasionally dispensed medicines. When none of these worked, illness was often ignored, leading to later complications and even death.

We used to hope that our sickness would go away, that it was only a temporary thing. A lost day in the fields meant loss of wages. I am sure some died because of leaving it too late.

The lack of legislative protection against dangerous working conditions and the absence of an adequate infrastructure such as inspectors and safety officers to enforce legislation where it did exist also left casualties in its wake. Injuries from farm machinery, pesticide poisoning and skin conditions from contact with hazardous chemicals regularly took place. At Tsoro and other tobacco farms another occupational hazard related to the sorting and packing of tobacco. The barns in which this was done accumulated large amounts of light dust which acted as an irritant when breathed in over long periods of time.

Mothers with young children on their backs would work for 8–9 hours a day, six days a week in those barns. The eyes of the children would be red and swollen. They would cough at night.

Ill health, poor living conditions, lack of education, no social amenities and an uncertain future had a tremendously demoralising impact on the farmworker population of Tsoro. It was often difficult to mobilise the community to do anything to improve their situation. Even when the farmer was later to provide bricks for construction of latrines and houses, or fencing and pipes for vegetable gardens, many workers indicated that they were not interested in contributing time and labour.

They used to say, 'Why bother improving our houses, digging gardens, constructing a borehole. We are only here for a short time. We would be doing it for someone else'.

The lethargy and frustration of those years translated into high levels of alcoholism which offered an unfortunate if understandable means of escape from their existence. Workers would run up debts to the farmer for consumption of alcohol which they would have to pay off through work. Others spent their savings on beer so that even if they wanted to leave they did not have the means to do so. 'The beerhall was the focus of all entertainment in our community,' Amai Raymond concluded.

Workers would spend most of their salaries on drink while the wife and children would go without food and clothing. There was a lot of domestic violence on the farm in those days and many broken marriages.

The curse of old age

From the census statistics of 1982 it was established that of the 1,600,000 people in commercial farming areas, over 5 per cent were in the age group of 60 years and over (Loewenson and Chinhori 1986, p65). For the majority of farmworkers old age held no prospect of an easier life or a comfortable retirement. Once their ability to work was diminished most were summarily dismissed with little or no compensation for a lifetime of effort they had often contributed to a particular employer.

Prior to independence and subsequent legislation which was brought in to enforce pension rights for permanent labour, there was no obligation on owners to provide end-of-term benefits for retired workers. Some voluntary schemes were in operation but inter-farm migration, illiteracy and lost records meant that many workers lost out on benefits due to their inability to prove payments. *Moto Magazine* (September 1983) reported the case of an old man who had worked on a commercial farm for most of his life. When he came to claim his pension he was told that the person who had made the arrangement was no longer there and that nothing could be done for him. A social security study in 1980, carried out by the Whitsun Foundation, claimed that only 1.1 per cent of permanent employees in the agricultural sector could expect pensions above the poverty datum line on retirement. Seasonal and contract workers had no entitlements whatsoever.

The lack of provision for old age was especially acute for migrant workers. Whereas the indigenous population who came from the communal lands had maintained contacts with their extended families and kin in these areas or retained a plot of land they could retire to, foreign workers did not have this safety net. Despite the fact that many of them had worked in Zimbabwe for most of their lives they lacked the ethnic ties and nationality rights needed to own land.

Many could not return to their own countries for a variety of reasons. Jonathan Kadandara wanted to return to Malawi, the place of his birth, but the prospect of accomplishing that journey home became more remote every year:

Amos Chipopa (left) and Luis Dimango (right) came from Mozambique to work in the commercial farms of northern Zimbabwe in the 1950s. Dismissed from employment after years of service they received little remuneration to help them in their old age. They now scrape a living on the impoverished soils of Muzarabani district, northern Zimbabwe.

I had no money. I lost contact with my family. And how could I return in these rags? I would have been ashamed returning like this.

After 40 years as a farm labourer he had nothing to show for that effort. At the end of his working life he received nothing in terms of a pension or allowance to help him during his old age. The salaries he received on the farms where he was employed were too meagre to save anything. Now he lives in a small mud hut on a farm in northern Zimbabwe that another family abandoned because of the leaking roof and eroded walls. If it wasn't for the help of other workers who gave him food he would probably have starved.

Civil war in neighbouring countries, social disruption and lost contact with families have also prompted migrant workers to stay behind. Some have managed to acquire a plot of land in the communal areas but these are often in the worst agricultural regions of the country, unwanted by anyone else. Amos Chipopa, who is over 60, came from Mozambique many years ago. He now lives with his wife and children in Muzarabani, an impoverished district of northern Zimbabwe where many of his compatriots ended up. The plot of land he has rented from the local chief is barely enough to keep himself and his family alive. Several years of drought meant almost negligible harvests. When the rains did come other problems developed. Amos has spent many of his nights out in his fields, throwing stones and banging tins to keep away the wild animals that raided his crops. 'Thirty years ago,' he claimed, 'it might have been different. I could have developed this land, planted more maize and put up a fence. But I left all my strength back there.'

'Back there' is on the commercial farms of northern Zimbabwe where Amos worked ever since he left Mozambique when he was a teenager. Eighteen of those years were spent on one farm where, established as a foreman, he thought he might settle. But when the farmer sold his property in 1976 the new owner did not want the old workforce. Amos was evicted and given nothing more than a few hundred dollars for the previous 18 years of work.

The lack of provision for old age was not only a personal tragedy for those affected but also created a climate of labour docility on the farms. Workers often refused to complain about excessive hours of work, unsafe conditions and poor housing for fear of losing the goodwill of the farmer and his help when their working lives were over. Those who were favoured received 'retainer' status, a small plot of land sufficient for their immediate needs, and a hut in the compound. But the majority could expect to end up with nothing, evicted as squatters to make way for the next family.

The pre-independence era can be summed up as a period of almost complete employer control over labour. It was a control supported and encouraged by the state in order to yield maximum profits from the commercial farming sector at the lowest possible cost. Their strength exhausted after years of work, its victims were discarded like bits of broken-down machinery when their usefulness was over. Interviewed shortly after independence, one worker summed up his frustration towards a system which had taken everything and given so little in return:

I have been working here since 1950 until today – with no pension, no bonus, no change in housing. My father worked on this farm until he died. I was born here in the same year as the farmer's son and now I work for him,· under the same conditions as my father worked for his father.[7]

---

7   *Moto Magazine*, no 43.

3
Constraints to change

In the early 1950s each white household had, on average, two African servants, and the number of automobiles per capita (one for every four whites) rivalled that of the United States. The average annual income of Africans in 1976 stood at the equivalent of US$150 whereas that of the Europeans approached US$8,000 (UNDP 1980, p*xiii*). Fearful of losing such economic privileges and status 260,000 whites (3.8 per cent of the population) continued to rule over 6,700,000 Africans (95.8 per cent) until 1980, well after most other countries on the continent had won their independence (Stoneman et al 1981, p37).

The relinquishment of political power took place only after a long and bitter armed struggle which over a ten-year period accounted for 20,000 lives, thousands of injured and disabled and the forced relocation of half a million black Zimbabweans by the government to prevent their support for the liberation armies. Independence was finally achieved after the opposition parties of Robert Mugabe's ZANU (PF) and Joshua Nkomo's ZAPU agreed at the Lancaster House talks in London in late 1979 to suspend the conflict in return for a transition to democracy. In the resulting general elections of March 1980 ZANU (PF) won with a convincing 63 per cent of the vote.

Yet independence was not attained without making major concessions to the previous regime. These were enshrined in the Lancaster House Agreement which restricted the new government's freedom in areas such as land redistribution and constitutional and legal reform. One of its major clauses prohibited government from solving the issue of inequitable distribution of land. Land could only be acquired from commercial farmers on a 'willing-buyer, willing-seller' basis and at competitive prices to be paid in hard currency if requested. The agreement also guaranteed a 20 per cent representation for whites in parliament for a further period of ten years, despite the fact that they constituted less than 4 per cent of the population.

For many black Zimbabweans, therefore, expectations at independence ran ahead of what was realistically possible. This was particularly true in the commercial farming sector where the continued economic power and political influence of European farmers set limits to substantial change. Fifteen years after 1980 the social conditions of farm labour continued to lag behind those of the rest of the country, a factor which has prompted criticism of government for its failure to enact the promises it made at independence to deal with this issue.[1] Yet without absolving the government of its responsibilities in this area it is important to understand the constraints, both internal and external to Zimbabwe, which set limits to what it could do. This chapter outlines some of these. As Jeff Herbst noted in his survey of Zimbabwean politics after the first decade of independence:

> *In 1980, ZANU (PF) did not gain control over a weak colonial state that had been hurriedly improved for Independence and on which they could quickly put their imprimatur (the typical scenario for countries that gained their independence in the 1960s). Nor did the guerrillas win an outright victory as Frelimo had done in Mozambique, where the old state collapsed creating a vacuum into which new government structures and practices could be placed. Instead, the Black government took over a bruised, but not defeated, settler state which contained powerful anachronistic elements that were hostile to the political project of the new regime.* (Herbst 1990, p30)

Economic power

At independence the commercial farming sector occupied a position of unrivalled economic pre-eminence in the country. This had been achieved through a coalition between farmers and the state that dated back to the formative years of colonial rule with land seizure and restrictive legislation on the indigenous population. One early state intervention was the policy of subsidised prices for agricultural products. This first took place in the 1930s when heavy government subsidies on maize rescued European farmers from a potentially disastrous slump on the world market. In order to attract white settlers to the land commercial farmers became the beneficiaries of a government system in the 1950s that set prices for many of their crops and guaranteed the purchase of these when they were marketed.

Agricultural loans were another example of massive state support. In 1978 the Agricultural Finance Corporation (AFC), which was set up to assist the agricultural sector, distributed a total of Z$58 million in credit. The entire amount went to commercial farmers and only in 1979 was a facility created to assist peasants in communal lands (Roussos 1988, p63). Although there have been changes thereafter commercial farms still receive 67 per cent of the total

---

1   The 1980 election manifesto of ZANU(PF) singled out commercial farmworkers as a group in particular need (ZANU(PF) 1980, p10).

value of loans and 200 times more credit per capita than peasant agriculture (Loewenson 1992, p63).

State provision of roads, electricity, irrigation and training also contributed to a situation whereby in 1980 commercial farmers had attained a level of economic leverage that was difficult for the new government to challenge. In 1978, 85 per cent of gross agricultural production came from commercial farms which produced all of the country's tobacco, tea, coffee, sugar and most of its cotton. Between 1978 and 1983 tobacco earned on average 46.5 per cent of Zimbabwe's total foreign exchange (Roussos 1988, p70).

Especially after witnessing the effects of the sudden imposition of revolutionary policies in neighbouring Mozambique, when independence from Portugal was achieved in 1975, the new government was anxious to avoid a similar flight of capital and expertise out of the country. Prior to the Lancaster House talks Samora Machel, then president of Mozambique, had warned the Zimbabwean liberation movements of the consequences of pursuing policies that would radically alter the economic status-quo. Portuguese settlers had fled Mozambique with their capital and influence leaving behind a devastated economy. With economic power so heavily entrenched in the commercial farming sector the new government in Zimbabwe was reluctant to antagonise farmers despite the conditions of labour which had made their wealth possible.

This economic influence of the commercial farming sector was further exaggerated by the role of international capital. Of particular concern to the government was the status of South Africa, as both investor and trading partner. In 1980 up to a third of total foreign capital stock and a quarter of total capital stock in the country was owned by South African companies. In 1986 35 per cent of Zimbabwean agriculture was still under their control (Herbst 1990, p114). Of these companies Anglo-American was the most powerful with extensive interests in mining, finance, property and manufacturing. Its agricultural interests included the Hippo Valley and Triangle estates, the major sugar producers in the country. The South African Imperial Cold Storage Ranch at Nuanetsi in the south of Zimbabwe covered over 400,000 hectares of land.

Fear of antagonising South African interests in agriculture was a major constraint on Zimbabwean policy in the post-independence period. This was not only to avoid possible disinvestment by these companies but economic retaliation, through either the blockage of exports and imports through South African ports and transport routes or the imposition of punitive tariffs on Zimbabwean goods destined for that market. South Africa demonstrated its economic muscle on several occasions. Most notoriously, in August and September 1981, as a retaliation for Zimbabwe's criticism of its apartheid policies, it withdrew transport facilities, depriving the Zimbabwean economy of fuel and an outlet for its agricultural exports. The transport crisis was said to have cost the country some Z$5 million per week in lost revenues (Hanlon 1986, p28).

Economic leverage has not only come from South Africa. Threats of international disinvestment and suspension of foreign aid have greeted occasional attempts by government to improve conditions for labourers in the agricultural sector. In 1985, for example, the government proposed to establish a new minimum wage of Z$143 per month for all agricultural workers. This took place in the wake of a boost in agricultural sales of some 47 per cent over the previous year. The move, however, was greeted by a storm of criticism from agro-industries, transnationals and individual farmers who cited bankruptcy as the consequence of such a stipulation. Yet the proposed wage rise still lagged behind the poverty datum line for an average family. In a survey carried out in Mashonaland West, Mashonaland Central and Masvingo provinces in 1985, average monthly earnings were found to be only a third of minimum subsistence needs. Nevertheless faced with the collective antagonism of agro-industry the government backed down and reduced the proposed minimum wage level by 50 per cent to Z$71 per month.

Political influence

Economic leverage was reflected in the level of political representation that this sector could draw upon to promote its interests both before and after independence. The government of Ian Smith's Rhodesia Front Party, which ruled the country from 1965 to 1980, was in effect a government of commercial farmers. This was reflected in its composition. Ten out of the 18 cabinet ministers in 1964 were large-scale commercial farmers, including Ian Smith who owned a ranching estate near Shurugwi in southern Zimbabwe. The Rhodesia Front formed the principal channel of white political representation in the post-independence period, winning the entire 20 white-allocated seats at successive elections until 1990 when the terms of the Lancaster House Agreement expired.

Commercial farmers not only penetrated senior levels of government but a whole variety of other institutions. Parastatals like the Agricultural Finance Corporation and the Grain Marketing Board, and marketing authorities like the Rhodesian Tobacco Corporation were either headed by European farmers or had coopted them on to their boards. These institutions continued beyond 1980 with an entrenched group of influential decision-makers antagonistic to substantial reform in the agricultural arena.

To this day commercial farmers also retain one of the most powerful and well-organised lobbying groups in the country. The Commercial Farmers Union (CFU) dates back to 1942 when it was founded as an organisation to make representation to government. The Rhodesian National Farmers Union, as it was then called, used its influence to have the government pass a licensing act which made it mandatory for all commercial farmers to buy a license from the newly formed union. This guaranteed a level of cohesion and financial resources which allowed the union to support a full-time annually elected president from among the farmers and a professional secretariat. The CFU has therefore been able to mount extremely sophisticated internal and external advertising campaigns, commission research and influence decision-makers in such areas as producer prices, minimum wages and land redistribution.

The CFU annual congress continues to be attended by senior government officials, including the Minister of Agriculture, providing a forum for farmers to influence government policy. CFU-sponsored tours of commercial farms by members of parliament have also helped to win them friends. On one such tour in 1985 the MPs commented that the visit 'had exposed them to the problems faced by farmers' (*Herald*, 23 April 1985, cited in Loewenson 1992, p89). No mention was made of the problems faced by farm labourers.

A measure of the international influence of the CFU was also evidenced over the recent issue of land redistribution. At a meeting of international donors and government ministers in Paris in 1992 to discuss Zimbabwe's aid requirements, donors quoted a letter they had received from the CFU attacking the government for its proposed policy on land reform. It was clear that donors sided with the CFU on this issue, signalling a warning that if government did not take account of their representations financial assistance could be threatened.

The other principal influence that provided a major block to reform, particularly in the area of improved conditions for farm labour, was the continuing control of local government in commercial farming areas by land owners. During the colonial period Rhodesia had developed a dichotomous system of local government, a structure which was to remain in place after independence. Communal lands came under district councils, which replaced the old system of native councils headed by European Native Commissioners. After independence these were run by bodies that were elected by the local population. This accountability ensured that the district councils became an efficient channel of services, such as health care, education, public transport and other facilities denied to the people before 1980. Administration of the commercial farming areas, however, rested with rural councils (RCs), election to which was contingent on ownership of property. This effectively disenfranchised the entire community of farmworkers as far as local government was concerned.

The rural councils were first formed in the 1920s when they were known as Road Councils and had the mandate of maintaining the infrastructure in European farming areas for commercial purposes. In 1966 the Rural Councils Act created the legal framework for the establishment of 43 rural councils covering the entire LSF area. These councils were also empowered to provide health care, education and other social amenities to the inhabitants of the area, a move which effectively absolved the government of that time from any responsibility for this provision. With no real obligation to provide these, rural councils reflected the priorities of their members and continued to concentrate on the upgrading of roads, the construction of bridges and the provision of electricity to farm owners' houses. This emphasis has continued in many rural councils to the present day. A Secretary in the Ministry of Local Government in 1986 noted that many people still consider the rural council to be no more than 'a glorified road council'. Another report in 1985 claimed that rural councils were more responsible for the development and maintenance of road networks in their areas than for health and education provision (Herbst 1990, p182).

Fear of antagonising European farmers and their overseas lobby seems to have slowed the pace of government reform in this area. Despite the fact that the rural councils are to be amalgamated with district councils at the time of writing, in an attempt to improve social service provision in the commercial farming areas, the government has hesitated to grant farm workers an electoral voice in local government. This means that they will continue to be dependent on others to identify their needs and will not have the electoral leverage of their counterparts in communal areas to remove those who fail to deliver their promises.

A fragmented workforce

The conditions under which farm labour was and continues to be maintained has created a fragmented workforce that is unable to articulate and lobby for its demands. This was different from the situation in communal areas where, despite the overcrowding, relocation of families and lack of facilities, communities maintained a certain cohesion and identity. The communal lands formed the main recruiting ground for the liberation movements as well as its principal base of support during the war. This debt guaranteed a level of government commitment in the post-independence era to deliver services and improvements that had formed a principal reason for the people's struggle.

By contrast farm labourers have not achieved an effective or unified voice. Part of the reason for this was the variety of backgrounds and circumstances that they came from. On a farm like Tsoro, for example, there were workers not only from different parts of Zimbabwe but from different countries in the region such as Mozambique, Malawi and Zambia. Amai Raymond lamented the absence of a community spirit:

> *There were some families we could not even talk to because they spoke a different language. It was difficult to get to know each other. Meetings were attended by some and ignored by others. The only thing we had in common was our labour.*

A further limiting factor has been the impermanence and seasonality of the workforce. This is a phenomenon that has increased since independence, ironically enough in the wake of government legislation to protect workers against discrimination. The Labour Relations Act of 1985 stipulated that in company with other employees, agricultural workers were entitled to pension rights, maternity benefits, protection against unfair dismissal, sick leave and certain minimum standards of safety at work. Yet, prior to the passage of this Act, farm-owners had begun to de-classify their employees from permanent to seasonal, contract, casual, special or part-time status, despite the fact that many of them had worked for the same employer year after year.[2] This declassification allowed employers to bypass the new Act since these categories of labour were not covered by its provisions.

Between 1974 and 1984 100,000 permanent jobs were lost in agriculture and although it is difficult to estimate the number of non-permanent workers that have made up for this shortfall, due to their invisibility in statistics, it is widely believed that their numbers have increased by a similar amount. A CFU survey in 1984, for example, revealed that seasonal labour employed at peak periods exceeded the number of permanent workers. In another survey in 1986 it was found that labour demand on farms in Mashonaland during peak periods of need were met by the contribution of women and children (Lowenson 1992, p51).

The range of labour classifications has allowed farmers to divide workers into two camps, which has compromised the unity of action that could increase pressure for change. Workers' committees, established on farms after government insisted that each workplace should have a committee to liaise with employers, are routinely composed of male permanent employees including the foreman and other favoured personnel who are sometimes more sympathetic to the farmer than to their own colleagues. Workers interviewed in 1985 claimed that the presence of the foreman at meetings led to intimidation of those who openly stated their position. The same survey reported that non-permanent workers felt actively marginalised by those in permanent employment and as a result hardly participated in the committees. 'We don't help each other in times of crisis. It is each man for himself', was a frequent observation during the survey (Loewenson 1992, pp91–92). With a vast pool of labour to choose from, especially in recent years with the large numbers of Mozambican refugees fleeing civil conflict and desperate for work, it is obvious that while farmers can easily

2   Classification of employment status of labour, 1983
   Permanent: Full employment. Monthly wages at above minimum levels, no dismissal without state/union consent.
   Non-permanent:
   1 Seasonal. Up to eight months continuous employment per year.
   2 Contract. Employed on a temporary basis to carry out piece/task work set by the employer.
   3 Casual. Up to six weeks continuous employment per three calendar months. Paid hourly/weekly.
   4 Special. Due to physical or mental disability, employed to do only part of the work of an able-bodied employee. Includes old-age workers.
   5 Part-time. Employed less than five hours per day or 30 hours per week, paid daily or weekly.

replace someone who complains, that person has few options to follow if he loses his job.

Union representation

The General Agricultural and Plantation Workers Union of Zimbabwe (GAPWUZ) was formed only after 1980 and co-existed for five years with other unions until its registration as a separate organisation in 1985. Much of its activity has focused on its own financial survival, since without government support it has no guaranteed form of income apart from workers' contributions. Yet recruiting its members, from both the permanent and non-permanent workforce on commercial farms, has been a slow and arduous struggle. Forty-eight field operators, who are located in each of the eight provinces of Zimbabwe, have regularly been refused access to compounds by farmers. They have also been faced with an unsympathetic labour force after some owners instructed workers to refuse union membership if they wished to retain their jobs.

Current membership figures are in the region of 25,000, which is only a fraction of potential numbers. Privately owned commercial estates with a highly mobile labour force and large migrant component have proved more difficult to unionise than agro-industrial estates owned by foreign companies. 'Multinationals probably can't afford the scandal of refusing union activities', claimed one GAPWUZ officer:

At the same time the labour force on these estates tends to be longer term, indigenous and more literate. Some of the small commercial farms in parts of Mashonaland, however, are run like feudal empires where the owner wields absolute power.

Despite its low membership, lack of resources and staff, GAPWUZ has managed to defend workers' interests on occasion. The union has challenged cases of unfair dismissal, inadequate compensation for injuries received at work and infringements of safety regulations on farms. In 1992 it successfully defended 25 workers on a farm near Harare who had been dismissed by the farmer on medical grounds. A doctor had falsely substantiated the owner's claim after being bribed, which allowed the farmer to dismiss them within the law. The union successfully overturned the ruling after receiving independent medical confirmation that the labourers were fit for work. A GAPWUZ officer admitted that for every successful case the union has prosecuted there are many more instances of unfair practice that it never hears about. But cases like the one above have helped raise the profile of GAPWUZ, and increasingly encouraged farm workers to approach it for representation.

Yet the union's overall strategy of worker education, lobbying for state support for farm labour and uniting its disparate elements remains unrealised. High levels of illiteracy and mobility mean that most workers are still ignorant about their rights. Public demands by the union for better wages, pension schemes, improved health care and educational provision, the right to vote at local government elections, housing off farmer's land for retired workers and an improved labour and safety inspectorate has not been adequately responded to by the state. As for unity, the divisions in the labour force between permanent and non-permanent workers, migrant and indigenous labour have prevented the realisation of the kind of solidarity that has won improvements for workers in other sectors of the economy. 'The union is only as strong as its members', claimed one GAPWUZ officer, 'and in order to compete against the professionalism, unity and organisation of the CFU we have a very long way to go.'

4
The commercial farm health workers programme

The government's hesitancy after independence in challenging the commercial farming sector and radically altering the social conditions of its labour force has left many people disappointed. But without excusing the continued impoverishment of a large section of the population it is important to understand some of the constraints faced by the new government. Not only did it confront a lobby of immense political and economic power, it also inherited a system that did not allow a rapid, coherent strategy to alter the status quo. Of the 11,000 senior officers in the civil service at independence only one third were African and none of these held positions above senior administrative level. Institutions which represented the economic power of European settlers, such as the Ministry of Agriculture, the Ministry of Labour and the Ministry of Mines retained a bias towards previous policies through decision-makers and bureaucrats who were resistant to change and who were well placed to sabotage government efforts if they wanted to. One author has claimed:

At independence the ZANU(PF) leadership constituted a thin veneer atop a largely untransformed state apparatus. The Cabinet found itself in a fragile position because institutions wholly or partly controlled by groups of dubious loyalty were interposed between the leadership and its popular base. (Bratton 1981, p452)

One institution, however, which did not have the conservative bias of other establishments was the Ministry of Health. Prior to 1980 this had functioned as a relatively minor department of government, reflecting the low priority accorded to health services for the majority of the population. Its rapid expansion in 1980 and the newness of the bureaucracy meant that it was Africanised much more quickly than other ministries and thus the government did not require so much centralised control in order to guarantee its allegiance to policies of equity and fairness. The Ministry of Health consequently evolved a decentralised structure of decision-making which allowed its officers at provincial and district level considerable scope to deal with the problems they came across.

Their task of rectifying a gross imbalance in the delivery of services was immense. By the time of independence the whites had developed a health care system for themselves that rivalled any that were available in developed western countries. The doctor–patient ratio for the European population stood at 1:830. There was one hospital bed for every 219 whites and the hospitals from which the black population were excluded until the mid-1970s had much the same equipment found in western medical institutions. Approximately Z$144 per year was spent on health care for each white in 1979.[1]

The contrast with the facilities and services available for the black population, especially the rural majority, was acute. The same 1979 survey revealed that in several provinces there was only one doctor for every 100,000 people. There was only one hospital bed for 525 black people and the facilities were of poor quality and overcrowded. Only Z$31 per year was spent on health care for each urban African and a meagre Z$4 on the care of each person in the rural areas.[2]

This disparity in health services exaggerated by the inequalities in socio-economic conditions had a direct bearing on the kinds of illness that both population groups suffered, as well as on their respective life expectancies. While the average European male could expect to live to 67, his African counterpart had a life expectancy of 49. Prior to 1980, the infant mortality rate among the white population was 17 per thousand live births (compared to 16 in Britain) and the disease pattern was identical to that seen in industrialised countries, with degenerative and stress disorders and cancer accounting for most fatalities. In contrast, blacks in Rhodesia had the typical health profile of the population of an impoverished third world country. Infant mortality stood at between 120 and 220 per 1000 live births, rivalling figures for the most deprived parts of the continent. Africans suffered extensively from malnutrition, and, reflecting their poor social conditions, diseases such as measles, tuberculosis, dysentery, malaria and bilharzia were common.

Determined to reverse both the racial imbalance in health provision and the emphasis on expensive curative care, the new Ministry of Health with substantially increased government funding announced its intention to deliver services to the neglected population of the communal areas.[3] One cornerstone of its strategy was the establishment of rural health centres which would form the base of a service pyramid extending from these to district to provincial then central hospital level.

---

1   See Gilmurray, J, et al, 1979. The struggle for health, Mambo Press, pp36–38. Also: Ministry of Health, 1984. *Zimbabwe, planning for equity in health*, Ministry of Health, Harare, p30.
2   For further discussion see Sanders, D, 'A study of health services In Zimbabwe' in UNDP 1980, p408.
3   During each of the first two years following independence, real actual expenditure of the Ministry of Health increased by approximately 33 per cent and 20 per cent respectively (see Chisvo 1992, p4). At the same time the amount of money allocated for expenditure on preventive services doubled from 1981 to 1982 and from 1982 to 1983. See: *Rebuilding Zimbabwe at 5 years of independence*, 1985, Mardon Printers, Harare, p218.

Rural health centres were to provide basic promotive, preventive, curative and rehabilitative care and were to serve a catchment population of approximately ten thousand people who should be within 8 kilometres (walking distance) of the facility. Included among its services were the delivery of uncomplicated births, routine immunisations, child health and nutrition, control of communicable diseases, basic dentistry and health and nutrition education. The centres were to be staffed by State Certified Nurses whose training was also to be modified to take account of their role as educators and health promoters. By 1985 210 new facilities had been constructed throughout Zimbabwe's eight provinces and a further 160 existing centres had been upgraded or reconstructed to fulfil their new role.[4]

The other strategy adopted by the Ministry of Health was to mobilise local communities in helping to eradicate the social, environmental and economic causes of diseases which affected them. Many of the medical problems that the rural population suffered in pre-independence Zimbabwe were due to such factors as contaminated water, poor sanitation, inadequate nutrition, low standards of hygiene, poor housing and ignorance of simple precautionary measures to guard the health of the family. In order to incorporate communities as active participants in changing these, the Ministry of Health established a cadre of health promoters to work with rural households.

The village health worker (VHW) programme was established in 1982 and centred on the training of workers appointed from among the rural communities where they would be based. The aim was to provide one VHW for every 500 to 1,000 people. Their role was to encourage rural communities to be self-reliant in the construction of latrines and protected wells and to promote basic hygienic standards. Within three years the programme had trained 3,800 VHWs in basic preventive, promotive and curative interventions. Within a period of five years over 40,000 Blair latrines (designed in Zimbabwe to prevent the spread of disease) had been constructed and 10,730 protected wells established throughout the country. The VHWs were paid an allowance by the state which guaranteed some continuity of service from those who had been trained.

As a result of the health-promoting activities of VHWs and the establishment of rural health centres the infant mortality rate in communal areas halved within a few years of independence and has further declined since.[5] Immunisation rates increased from less than a quarter of all rural children in 1980 to three-quarters in 1986 (Ministry of Health 1987). Malnutrition among under-fives also showed a dramatic decrease of 50 per cent within four years of the ministry programme. A communal farmer in Mashonaland West province compared the services that are available now with the deprivations of the pre-independence years:

---

4   Ministry of Health, 1985. *Zimbabwe, Health For All – Action Plan*, Ministry of Health, Harare, p186.
5   See Agere, S, 'Progress and problems in the health care delivery system' in Mandaza et al 1986, p372.

In the old days the nearest hospital or clinic was over a day's journey away. We used to pray that an illness in the family was not too serious. I remember some people dying on the journey to hospital. Now we have a nearby clinic with a nurse, a better transport system, a borehole with clean water and knowledge of how to prevent the problems that earlier affected us. Our lives have definitely changed. Illness is no longer the disaster it used to be.

In company with their counterparts in communal land areas, commercial farmworkers in 1980 suffered a similar if not worse deprivation in health care provision. A survey carried out between 1980 and 1981 revealed an incidence on commercial farms of diarrhoeal diseases, respiratory tract infections, tuberculosis, malaria, measles and malnutrition that was among the worst in the country.[6] In Mashonaland Central province, with its large number of commercial farms and labour-intensive agriculture, conditions for workers were sufficiently appalling to prompt the Provincial Medical Director (PMD) to establish a pilot project in the farming area around Bindura, the administrative capital of the region.

It would be wrong to claim that the FHW programme arose out of a strategic plan to rectify the conditions of farm labour in Zimbabwe after independence. Resource constraints within government and the belief that farm owners should bear the responsibility for the welfare of their workers meant that there was no similar grand design of the kind that informed health programmes in communal areas.

A union official acknowledged that the government had been placed in something of a dilemma. If it were to build a clinic or school, provide better water and sanitation facilities or improved worker housing on private property the value of that estate would be substantially increased. As a result the selling price would be higher if the property came on the market, and since government itself was interested in acquiring commercial farms for resettlement purposes it was reluctant to contribute to the higher costs it might then have to pay. One provincial health official noted: 'Commercial farmers were seen as responsible for rural councils and government did not want to be seen as subsidising commercial farmers in what was seen as their duty to their employees.' (Herbst 1990, p184).

The decentralisation of the health services from head office in Harare to provincial level did allow PMDs who administered health care in the eight regions of Zimbabwe considerable latitude to implement programmes in response to the needs that they identified.[7] The origin of the FHW scheme was in such an

---

6　See Chikanza, I et al, 1981. 'The health status of farmworker communities in Zimbabwe', *Central African Journal of Medicine*, Vol 27, No 5, pp155–169.
7　Wrote Herbst: 'In the end the PMD has the ultimate say. A Mashonaland PMD confirmed this view and said that head office approves PMD decisions automatically because it is the PMD who has the knowledge of the area in which the health centre will be built. Civil servants in the Ministry Of Health's head office confirm that the primacy of the PMD is not just theory.' (Herbst 1990, p176).

initiative arising in a specific region of Zimbabwe through the concern of the PMD and other health personnel in that area.

Looking back on the initial years of the project the FHW programme in Bindura seems partly a matter of experimentation whose very lack of strategy possibly allowed it to evolve more flexibly than if it had been tied to a more comprehensive plan. ICD health workers, recruited from the UK to the province, acknowledged that they had much to learn in delivering an appropriate, sustainable and participative service to a community characterised by its fragmented and submissive nature. Health service personnel had to expand their skills in community development and mobilisation, learn health education techniques appropriate for their audience, and practice diplomacy in dealing with farmers who were sometimes reluctant to allow them on to their property.

At the same time as new areas of need began to be identified within farmworker communities that would improve their health but did not come under the particular brief of the ministry, the importance of donor assistance also became apparent. For ministries whose services were tied to a very specific area, the latitude to fund and support alternative types of assistance was restricted. The willingness of international donors to develop literacy work, income generation, the creation of women's clubs, home and garden competitions, and so on within the scheme added an important complement to the input of Ministry of Health staff in their own areas of expertise.

While one might criticise the seemingly haphazard development of the FHW scheme described in the following pages and its process of trial and error, an argument can also be made for the value of not constricting development programmes in too rigid a blueprint. Strategies formulated in advance by planners can often compromise the willingness to take account of the wishes and capacities of those they are supposed to help. Project beneficiaries then become objects of charity who are seen as the recipients of services rather than participants in their own development. Given the fact that the service infrastructure in commercial farms (clinics, schools, adequate accommodation, clean water) could not be provided by the state and was unlikely to be adequately supported by owners, any programme which did not encourage active farmworker participation would have made very few inroads in improving their conditions. The time taken to explore ways of encouraging this contribution was an invisible part of the programme yet it was as important as all the direct, tangible inputs such as mobile health clinics, immunisation programmes and provision of medicines that were also made.

The programme in Bindura

The Bindura project began in 1981 and aimed to train workers on farms along similar lines as the VHWs in communal areas. These were to be called farm

Farmworkers in Mashonaland Central mould bricks for the construction of latrines.

health workers or FHWs. In order to promote community involvement, project staff visited each of the farms that were initially targeted to explain to the workforce the aims of the programme. The community was then invited to select a female member for a four-week training course that was to take place in Bindura. The FHW's role was primarily envisaged as an educative one. It was her task to create awareness of health issues among the community members and mobilise them to change certain aspects of their behaviour in order to improve their health. This included the digging of pit latrines, the establishment of vegetable gardens for nutritional purposes, and improved hygienic practice around the home. In the absence of a regular nurse or accessible clinic the FHW was also asked to provide a simple, curative service. Patients with more serious conditions were to be referred on for more professional attention. During their initial visits, project staff had also realised that the health of children was compromised by a lack of care and supervision while their mothers were working. FHWs were, therefore, also given the task of establishing pre-schools on the compounds.

Even at this early stage it was realised that health needs of the community required a broader range of inputs than the regular visits of a doctor or nurse. A pre-school trainer as well as a builder were therefore added to the outreach team that visited the community once a month. The role of the builder was to provide advice and assistance in the construction of latrines and the protection of water supplies. Yet it was not just project staff that came to realise that simple health interventions were not enough. Communities themselves also began to identify their poverty, lack of income and insecure status as contributory causes of the illnesses that afflicted them. One request that was increasingly heard on project farms was for information concerning employment rights and labour organisation. In response, some efforts were made to create awareness of the functions and purpose of trade unions which affected the workers.

By 1983 108 FHWs had been trained from the 200 farms in the project area. An evaluation carried out by the Department of Community Medicine in the University of Zimbabwe (Loewenson et al 1983) noted significant improvements in many areas:

- Immunisation rates had increased on farms with FHWs from 17 per cent to 81 per cent in the intervening two-year period.
- More women attended ante-natal clinics.
- A high proportion of mothers had learned to use oral rehydration solution when their children had diarrhoea, a major killer on commercial farms.
- There were improvements in nutritional status.
- The evaluation indicated an improvement in the construction of sanitation facilities on farms with FHWs: 59 per cent of workers had access to latrines in 1983 compared to 15 per cent in non-project farms.
- Pre-schools were felt to be a valuable asset by both farmers and workers and were attended by 43 per cent of children. They also provided an opportunity for health workers to screen children on a regular basis and implement supplementary feeding where necessary.

Yet the programme was not without its difficulties and contradictions. One issue that compromised the effectiveness of the scheme was that of sustainability. The FHW programme arose in response to very obvious needs but it lacked the firm commitment of government and farm owners to support it. Each claimed that the major responsibility for the welfare of workers should rest with the other. The refusal of government, for example, to pay the allowances of FHWs resulted in confusion as to who should do so. Some received nothing. Others received a wage either from the farmer or from the community through profits from beer sales. Since this was often less than what they could earn in the farmer's fields many FHWs either terminated their work with the project or suspended their health promotion activities during times when labour demand was high.

It was partly because of this kind of resource need that international NGOs were asked by the programme initiators to support the project. Thus Save the Children Fund (UK) contributed transport and driver costs for outreach work as well as training support for the FHWs selected to come to Bindura. It has been argued that the involvement of international NGOs absolved farm owners from meeting their responsibilities in terms of the welfare of their workers. Yet confronted with the often appalling health problems that afflicted such communities, the alternative of refusing assistance would have been worse.

At the same time, while it was largely humanitarian concern that prompted their involvement in the first place, the programme itself did offer scope for more development-oriented activities. From its inception the FHW programme was conceived as an educational initiative, aiming to provide farmworker communities with a basis of knowledge and confidence to allow them to tackle some of their own problems. It did not directly provide improved accommodation, protected wells or nutritional gardens but lobbied farmers to come up with the materials and the community to provide the labour to realise these improvements. Furthermore, the space that was created within the programme to engage in community development expanded the possibilities of assistance to much more than a simple health intervention. As the 1983 evaluation concluded, many of the structural causes behind ill health still needed to be tackled. Poor housing and overcrowding, low wages, lack of schools, unsafe working conditions and inadequate job security continued to have a detrimental effect on farm workers' well-being. Strengthening the ability of these communities themselves to press for change in such areas provided the rationale for much of the later assistance that was given.

Programme expansion and diversification

The 1983 evaluation indicated sufficient improvements in the health of communities on project farms to convince the Ministry of Health and its project partners to expand their activities. Thus in 1984 an agreement was signed with the rural councils of Mvurwi, Shamva and Mazoe in Mashonaland Central province to implement programmes in their respective commercial farming areas. This project was assisted with funds from SCF and the United Nations Development Programme (UNDP). In 1987 the scheme was extended to an additional four rural council areas in the province: Centenary, the northern part of Bindura called Matepatepa, Glendale and Concession.

Rural councils were involved in the programme for several reasons. As the local authority in the commercial farming areas, they were responsible for coordinating development programmes. Despite their bias towards road construction and bridge building and their neglect of health care and education for the farmworker community they did provide an administrative and resource structure to ensure the continuity of programmes beyond the period of direct donor assistance. At the same time, because rural councils enjoyed the sympathy of farm owners, programmes supported by rural councils were more likely to be accepted by farm owners than those run by ministries which some saw as hostile to their interests. The project had ample evidence that without the good wishes of the farmer, improvements for the workers were almost impossible to achieve. Consequently a major effort was made to win the support of the rural council

Josephine Mutandiro, Save The Children Fund (UK) programme officer for Mashonaland Central province, addresses commercial farmers, rural council officials and other Ministry personnel at a meeting in Centenary to discuss the problems facing labour in the district.

through the holding of meetings and workshops to explain the benefits of the programme. Support was also given in terms of finance and training of personnel to help extend the rural council structure to accommodate other activities, such as income generation and literacy promotion on the farms.

Yet it was not only the agreement of farmers and the support of the authority that most represented their interests that was crucial to the development of the programme. The issue of community accountability also had to be tackled. Josephine Mutandiro, a programme officer with the Save the Children Fund (SCF) closely involved with the FHW scheme since its early years, indicated the importance of ensuring some element of community ownership of the project:

> *We did not want the FHW to be imposed from outside the community or to be solely answerable to other structures than the ones on the farms. This would have undermined the level of participation that was a major objective of the programme.*

Although the health teams indicated the recommended criteria of selection such as literacy, respect within the community, evidence of a good home environment, farm workers made the final choice of those to be trained.

Community accountability was also strengthened through the answerability of the FHW to the workers' committee, the main structure on the compound to address grievances between the workers and the owner. Workers' committees retained the right of dismissal if the FHW did not perform satisfactorily. They also formed the principal channel of communication between the FHW and the farmer if improvements to the compound or other health-related activities were suggested. But as Josephine Mutandiro acknowledged, committees on the farms needed strengthening in order to assume a more adequate supervisory role as well as a bargaining position in relation to the employer. Furthermore, structures of accountability had not been clearly articulated so that committees often operated independently of the real wishes of workers and their families. The marginalisation of women and seasonal labourers was reflected in their frequent exclusion from this group.

Yet it was the only structure on the compound that we could work through. We decided to see if we could improve the way it operated. To this end courses in leadership, community participation, record keeping, management and administrative skills for key people in these committees were organised.

(Josephine Mutandiro, SCF)

By 1987 some 491 FHWs had ben trained in the project areas, meeting a target of 60 farms for each rural council district in each of which two FHWs would be located. The course had now been lengthened from four to eight weeks and included an increasing community development component. FHWs were exposed to community mobilisation techniques which included the use of drama and song as well as the production of appropriate materials for health education. The composition of the mobile team was also altered to include officers from the Ministry of Community Development who had the role of encouraging income-generating projects among women on the farms as well as training in community cooperation and leadership skills.

Part of the reason for this new emphasis in the programme had been the disappointing levels of community participation in previous years. Self-reliance had been central to health care programmes in other parts of the country. In district council areas a politically mobilised peasantry with voting rights to local government and ownership of the land they lived on had eagerly assisted in the construction of clinics, wells and other environmental improvements. This had shifted some of the costs on to the community, allowing a wider distribution of resources as a result. The same level of participation had not taken place on farms. Insecurity of tenure, non-ownership of property, and weak social organisation restricted worker participation. Project planners realised that this was something of a vicious circle. Real community involvement was difficult because of the above limiting factors yet these would never change if farm workers themselves did not begin to challenge them through their own collective efforts.

The realisation of the importance of community empowerment also modified the timescale of NGO involvement. Working with communities as disadvantaged

Health-promotion drama on disability performed on a commercial farm near Centenary.

as those of farm workers demanded a level of patience and commitment that could not be limited to a standard two-to-three-year project cycle, the usual timescale of donor support. Despite its original intention, therefore, to limit assistance to a two-year project phase in each area, SCF programme officers felt that the awakening demands of the people it had helped mobilise on the farms needed to be further encouraged and developed rather than abandoned as soon as they arose. Consequently the organisation continued its involvement with the programme in Mashonaland Central through employing the services of three full-time officers whose role it was to promote community initiatives on the farms. In addition it funded coordinators in each project area to assist communities with income generation, cooperative development, the organisation of women's clubs and savings clubs and leadership training for worker's committees. To cater for the increasing demand for literacy on farms, SCF also provided salaries for three District Literacy Coordinators to monitor and support the training activities of literacy tutors drawn from within the farm community.

An increasing area of health work that also arose during this time centred around the issue of disability. High levels of malnutrition, poor ante-natal care, low standards of cleanliness and hygiene and the consequent prevalence of diseases such as tuberculosis and polio were common in many rural areas of the country, including on commercial farms. These resulted in levels of disability which one survey in 1983 estimated to affect one in ten of the rural population. Yet a serious shortage of qualified therapists and the absence of clinics and referral points had meant that many people with disabilities were left without assistance of any kind.

Children at a pre-school on a commercial farm with the farm health worker. The pre-school was constructed with financial assistance from the farmer, and labour of the workers.

Realising that a disability service along western lines, with a heavy emphasis on institutions and professional therapists, was impracticable given the magnitude of the problem and the scarcity of financial resources and qualified personnel, the Ministry of Health adopted a community-based approach towards rehabilitation. This involved a process of encouraging families and communities to share some of the responsibility of caring for their disabled through the provision of training and support in simple, rehabilitative techniques. Part of the role, therefore, of ICD therapists recruited to Mashonaland Central province was to provide such an input to farmworker communities. This also involved the training of FHWs in early identification of childhood disabilities for referral to the district or provincial services, increasing the chances of a more successful intervention than if diagnosis was made at a later stage.

The FHW programme in other provinces

FHW programmes began to be implemented in other areas in 1984 after the pilot project results were nationally circulated. Most of these schemes were started in similar labour-intensive agricultural regions of Mashonaland West, Mashonaland East and Manicaland where training centres were established. The responsible implementing authority varied within each region from wholly Ministry of Health in some areas to wholly rural council control in others.

Surveys of these programmes revealed similar problems to those that had occurred in Mashonaland Central. Drop-out of FHWs after training was high, reaching 40 per cent in some areas of Mashonaland West. Non-payment of allowances, movement of husbands to other farms and rejection by the community were some of the reasons cited to explain this phenomenon.

As more needs began to be revealed in farmworker communities, the activities of FHWs expanded from their initial role as health promoters. Community development activities, pre-school organisation and teaching were added to another demand by farmers and workers for a more comprehensive curative service. Officials from the Mashonaland West programme, at a review meeting held in 1986, stressed the need for more rigorous selection criteria for nominated candidates from the farms. Literacy and minimum educational qualifications were regarded as essential, although some participants pointed out that these were often available among younger women only, who would lose out in terms of the authority and respect accorded to older members of the community. In order to ensure that the investment in training was not wasted, the meeting also stressed the importance of obtaining the prior commitment of the farmer and community for payment of the FHW. Due to the collapse of services on some farms where only one worker had been trained it also recommended a minimum of two FHWs per community.

Poor promotion of the programme was also felt to be a problem. Farmers complained of a lack of information about the role of health workers on their compounds, although programme officers also commented that this was often due to their unwillingness to listen. Yet there was a strong consensus among programmes that since the acceptance of the farmer was crucial to the success of the scheme, more lobbying had to be done to solicit their support. This included establishing contacts with their representational bodies such as the CFU and the Tobacco Growers Association. One evaluation of an FHW programme concluded:

The success or failure of the scheme depends primarily on how much the farmer supports it. A concerted effort needs to he made to persuade farmers of the benefits of the FHW so that they make the necessary investment to improve environmental conditions.   (Warndorff 1990, p2)

Yet despite these problems, FHW initiatives realised sufficient improvements on commercial farms to prompt the Ministry of Health to promote a further development to the programme in 1990. With funding from SIDA (Swedish International Development Agency) it announced a national programme for farmworkers, in order to coordinate and rationalise some of the activities that had arisen in different project areas.

Acknowledging its debt to the pioneering developments of the Mashonaland Central programme, the policy document outlined its objective of expanding and establishing an FHW scheme in all of the eight provinces of Zimbabwe. The long-term objectives to be achieved through this approach were to make health care services more available to farmworkers and their families, to improve their nutritional status, with a particular emphasis on mothers and children and to further community participation (of both farm owners and farmworkers) in identifying and solving existing problems. The strategy adopted to achieve these included:

1   the conscientisation of the relevant personnel at national, provincial and district level, as well as in the rural councils and within the farming community itself;
2   the selection of people to be trained as FHWs by the workers' committees;
3   the training of the people selected, either in existing VHW training centres or at farm health training centres where these existed.

Since the announcement of the national programme a total of 1,074 FHWs have been trained, two per farm, across Zimbabwe's eight provinces, including 100 from the previously neglected farming areas of Matabeleland in southern Zimbabwe. With its higher proportion of farms, Mashonaland has had the bulk of these, some 900 out of the entire total trained in this two-year period. Although some of the newer programme areas still have considerable numbers of farms without an FHW, districts which have been within the scheme for a longer period have most of the estates covered. For example, of a total of 250 farms in the Mazoe region, 75 have two FHWs per farm, 150 farms have one and only 25 still have none.

In addition to expanding the training a standard syllabus has also been created in an attempt to achieve some unity across provinces so that mobility of FHWs will not compromise their effectiveness or acceptance in other areas. Two national workshops have also been held (in 1990 and 1992) which were attended by Ministry of Health personnel, rural council representatives and members of farmers' associations such as the CFU. Both were designed to outline the aims of the programme, to promote its acceptance among the farming community and improve the linkages between health personnel and rural council officers.

Before going on to discuss some of the issues that the FHW programme has still to confront, the next chapter gives a more concrete picture of the development of the scheme on a particular farm. Although the successes that have been registered at Dendere in Centenary district cannot be claimed by every establishment in Mashonaland Central province, the history of its involvement with the scheme is sufficiently representative of the author's findings at other locations to warrant its inclusion here.

5

The programme on Dendere farm

Thirty kilometres from Tsoro is Dendere farm, one of the first estates to be included in the Centenary district FHW programme. It has a similar profile to other farms in the area with a heavy concentration on tobacco production requiring a labour force of around 500, swelled by seasonal workers during times of need. Rebecca Goma, who has lived there for the past 25 years, was chosen by her community to be trained as a farm health worker in 1987.

She recalls the time when the health team from Centenary arrived in their compound announcing the establishment of a programme in their district. In a series of discussions with the community they were informed that this new initiative would help change their lives. At that time Dendere was little different from other farms in the area. The children were malnourished. Workers were continually ill. The conditions of their houses and the compound were poor, with few latrines, no running water and no facilities for children when mothers were working. But the visitors were not there to offer them quick solutions or provide them with free assistance and handouts. The community was told that the main agent of change would be themselves, that the principal effort would come from them. They were asked to select two women to be trained as FHWs to promote the programme in Dendere. Rebecca recalls:

The two of us had only a few years of schooling. We knew very little about health and the causes of illness on our farm. But what we lacked in education we made up for in our willingness to learn.

The training at the Centenary Rural Health Centre, for the 20 women who attended, lasted eight weeks. Rebecca learnt how to identify and treat common ailments such as diarrhoea, eye infections, scabies, influenza, simple burns and injuries. She was shown how to diagnose more serious problems such as malaria and sexually transmitted diseases, in order to be able to refer patients on to the nearest clinic or mobile health team. But Rebecca remembers most the emphasis

Women on Dendere farm display their vegetable garden which provides an added nutritional supplement to the diet of their families.

placed on preventive health measures as the most important part of the instruction she was given:

> We were taught to identify the basic factors behind the ill health that affected our communities. These were things we had not previously thought about. The importance of good housing, proper food, clean water and sanitation was made clear to us both through lectures and by visiting places where such improvements had taken place. It was our role to identify the source of a health problem and mobilise the community to do something about it.

The early years of the programme in Dendere, however, were not easy. The farmer remained to be convinced of the value of an FHW and it was only when conditions on the compound began to improve through their own efforts that he began to contribute with the provision of building materials for latrines, the installation of boreholes for clean water and the allocation of land for vegetable gardens. Rebecca also recalls some problems of initial acceptance within the community. The fact that FHWs were women operating within a conservative, patriarchal society caused difficulties. At meetings to discuss health-related issues they were often challenged by men who questioned their ability to offer advice:

> It had nothing to do with whether what we said was right or wrong. Simply because it came from a section of the community who were normally silent and usually accepted what our men told us it was open to disagreement.

At the same time the provision of a forum for women to discuss the reasons behind ill health of their families led to conflict. As they began to understand the consequences of under-nutrition and poor living conditions, demands were made on husbands to contribute a larger part of their time and salaries to the upkeep of the family, and less to the beerhall. As a result some men were reluctant to allow their wives to attend such discussions. On occasion they lobbied the husbands of the FHWs to 'control their wives'. There is still occasional friction, Rebecca confirms, but once conditions in the home improved, when children had better health, when families spent less money on medical bills, men saw the positive results of the women's work and became more supportive.

Another problem that the FHWs encountered was the reluctance among members of the community to change their perceptions about health and the causes of disease and illness. They did not believe that improvements in housing and living standards, better diet and nutrition, clean water and latrines were an answer to their problems. They claimed that what was needed was more doctors, a nearby clinic and a pharmacy. While the demand for expanded curative services was a legitimate one, Rebecca acknowledged, the possibility of this happening in the area was remote and so she had to convince people that there was more they could do for themselves.

A more difficult attitude to change was the fatalism that had developed among some of the workers. They would say, 'Illness has always been with us and always will be. There is nothing we can do about it'. Changing beliefs that have become so entrenched is a long and slow process, claimed Rebecca. It is something that cannot be forced, that no amount of lectures or admonitions from health workers will change. She remembers the impatience sometimes displayed by nurses visiting the farm, their irritation that things were not going as quickly as they had hoped:

But when people begin to see that their neighbours have good health, a higher income, more educated children as a result of their own efforts, they will be motivated to copy them. Setting an example is worth more than any words.

The principle of utilising existing structures and practices on the farm, rather than rejecting these out of hand and possibly losing community support, also necessitated their working alongside traditional healers and birth attendants. Health education programmes planned by doctors trained in western-style medicine had often ignored their possible contribution, especially in the pre-independence era when local healers were dismissed as primitive and dangerous. Traditional medicine was treated with scorn by the colonial authorities, agreed a former President of the Zimbabwe National Traditional Healers Association (ZINATHA), an organisation founded in 1981 to promote and register the estimated 30,000 traditional healers operating in the country. The activity of n'angas, derisively labelled witchdoctors by early settlers, was one of the first things to be prohibited by the colonial government in the late 1890s through the Suppression of Witchcraft Act. This was not because of an enlightened altruism towards the indigenous population, since alternative medical services for the majority were rarely provided:

It was more to do with the realisation that our traditional healers were the custodians of culture and tradition and a possible source of opposition to colonial rule. The legacy of dismissal has unfortunately continued to the present day among many health workers who have been taught to believe that the western system of medicine excluded the contribution of others.

Yet as Rebecca confirmed, the majority of the people on the farm usually consulted traditional healers and, in the days when almost no medical services were available at all, it was traditional birth attendants who supervised maternal deliveries. Consequently their position of authority and respect within the community necessitated a close working relationship so that their own contribution and suggestions would be accepted. Health mobilisation meetings, therefore, were not conducted without their attendance. Two traditional birth attendants (TBAs) on Dendere farm were also given a two-week supplementary training at the nearby rural health centre to improve their knowledge of hygiene, nutrition, pre- and post-natal care, delivery and identification of problem maternity cases for referral. In 1989 57 per cent of women delivering at home on commercial farms had the assistance of an upgraded TBA in Mashonaland Central province, as opposed to only 15 per cent two years previously.

Rebecca sums up her assessment of the FHW programme as a process of expanding options for the community. Initially she expected the focus of the scheme to be narrowly concentrated on the diagnosis of certain common ailments among workers and their families and their treatment either by herself or by referral to the health team that would visit them. But exploring the factors behind the ill health they suffered from has expanded their priorities into other areas that were never envisaged when they first started in 1987.

In order to supplement their income, women on Dendere farm have come together to set up projects:

We have always been dependent on the farmer or our husbands for the money we need to look after our families. But if the season is bad or the pay is poor it is always our health that is first to suffer. We decided that we had to help ourselves since no one else would do it for us. Now we have several projects that benefit both the community and ourselves.

One of these has not only provided an added income for its members but

Rebecca Goma (2nd from right) displays the soap-making project that has provided a group of women on Dendere farm with an added income.

benefitted the health of workers and their families. With a start up grant from International Cooperation for Development (ICD), Rebecca and several other women established a lucrative soap-making project after they identified a shortage on both their own compound and other farms in the surrounding area. This not only brings them money but has improved general cleanliness and hygiene. The incidence of scabies on the compound has decreased since the project began.

Part of ICD's rationale in supporting their request was that it had arisen as their own initiative. The women involved with the project had established a market for their product, had acquired the appropriate skills in soap manufacture and had sufficient evidence of past community action as to merit further support. These factors ensured that ownership of the project was firmly in their own hands and that it had not been prompted by an act of charity dependent on a donor for its motivation and implementation. It was in running projects like these themselves, claimed Rebecca, that people acquire the confidence and learn the skills to tackle other problems in their environment.

In order to run such projects effectively, the members also realised that they required other skills in literacy, numeracy and book-keeping. Dendere now boasts an active literacy group. Because of its new focus on an ability which will help them supplement their incomes it has attracted a more enthusiastic membership than when it was initially established and workers were unsure of how it might help them. Literacy has also been acknowledged by increasing numbers of

A literacy class in progress. Demand for literacy on farms has increased as workers begin to run income-generating projects which require reading, writing and numeracy skills.

women as a factor in promoting good health. Mothers have realised that they need to read the immunisation cards of their children. They need to know when to attend clinics for follow-up visits. They need to be able to read prescription details on their bottles of medicine. Workers need to read the warnings printed on bags of fertiliser and pesticides or the operating instructions on dangerous machinery.

The district literacy coordinator in Centenary, employed by the Ministry of Education but assisted with transport by SCF, agreed that relating literacy to the background and needs of the trainees was crucial. Many of the older materials were irrelevant to the situation of farmworkers. Because of their complaints and the high rate of non-attendance at classes, the Ministry of Education, with overall responsibility for literacy, recently produced a set of booklets on such issues as the factors behind ill health on farm compounds, the importance of immunisation, safety at work and labour regulations and workers' rights. Combined with the expanded programme of support offered to tutors on the farms by the literacy coordinators, rates of attendance have increased, as have the number of estates where programmes have started.

Yet despite these improvements, the coordinator commented, demand has outpaced the level of services offered to farm workers. In 1990 some 64 per cent of workers on commercial farms in the Mvurwi district of the province were assessed as illiterate. Of these, 97 per cent expressed their desire to attend literacy classes, yet only 12 per cent of the farms in the district had established any kind of programme. Problems of transport for literacy coordinators, their inability to cover both communal and commercial areas due to constraints of time and numbers, poor rates of pay and high mobility of tutors drawn from the community itself were some of the factors that continued to hamper the development of the programme.

Despite obstacles such as these and other limiting factors to do with their environment and working conditions, Rebecca points to the positive achievements that have taken place since 1987. She recalls some of the results of the survey carried out three years later which chronicled the improvements in health among families in Dendere and other estates in the district over the course of the FHW programme (Warndorff 1990). The incidence of diarrhoea in children under five years old had decreased from 44 per cent to 17 per cent. Malnutrition in the same age-group had dropped from 27 per cent of the children to 18 per cent. Immunisation figures had risen from 53 to 91 per cent of children. Families without a latrine had fallen from 64 per cent to 47 per cent. A refuse pit was now found in the majority of households as opposed to only 13 per cent of homes in 1987. The utilisation of pot racks had risen from 67 per cent to 81 per cent of families. Pre-schools had been established on 72 per cent of the farms in the district compared to only 6 per cent in 1987. Clubs were functioning in one of every three farms with one or more income-generating projects in each group.

Rebecca now displays with pride the neat houses and swept yards of the families in her compound, the soap-making project that brings them money, the vegetable gardens that supplement their diet with more nutritious foods. Although newcomers are not forced to participate or conform, community pressure is such that they would be made to feel unpopular if they did not display a commitment to maintaining standards that have now been achieved. That pressure, she claims, is evidence of the beginning of a new community spirit on the farm that was not there before, something that can be built upon to promote other changes and improvements: 'We have made the first step. The next one should be easier'.

6
Assessing the FHW programme – problems to overcome

A comprehensive evaluation of the FHW programme across all regions of Zimbabwe is difficult for several reasons. Firstly the scheme has only been introduced to some provinces (such as Midlands and Matabeleland) very recently, and has not had the length of time to develop beyond an initial, exploratory phase. At the same time, despite the announcement of a national plan in 1990, there is little real uniformity across regions, but considerable variation in terms of implementation and management. Furthermore, the vast bulk of primary research on the FHW programme has concentrated on its original project area where indeed most of its developments have been spearheaded. It is for these reasons, as well as the fact that the majority of the author's interviews and visits were conducted in Mashonaland Central province, that this assessment of the FHW programme is largely concerned with its activities there. Where surveys and statistics do relate to other provinces, however, these have been indicated.

The same survey of 1990 quoted by Rebecca Goma in the previous chapter indicated that improvements in farmworker status needed to be balanced against the failure of the programme to solve other issues. The fact that it had no powers of enforcing certain minimum standards in relation to accommodation and living environments, nor the resources to achieve these itself, limited major changes to the farmworkers' compounds. Despite efforts of workers to improve the appearance of their housing, the quality of accommodation was still poor, with over 65 per cent of households living in mud and thatch huts. Although the provision of boreholes had increased, the number of points was low, with families having to queue for long periods to fetch water. The lack of concrete run-offs allowed stagnant pools to collect around taps, providing a continuing source of infection on compounds. The quality of latrines was also questioned, with only 23 per cent of households having flush toilets. Many of the latrines that had been constructed were of poor quality and did not conform to the recommended Ministry of Health standards in relation to design and materials. National statistics revealed a similar picture overall. A survey carried out by the Ministry of

A typical watering point on a commercial farm near Centenary, northern Zimbabwe. The absence of a concrete run-off has allowed stagnant pools of water to form, providing a breeding ground for mosquitoes and communicable diseases.

Health in 1991 indicated the ratio of brick to mud housing on commercial farms countrywide at 30:70 per cent. Only 7.9 per cent of farmworkers had access to treated tap water (Auret 1992, p53).

The continuing reluctance of the farm owner to make significant capital investments to improve workers' living conditions is the main reason for the slow pace of progress in this area. In their defence, farmers interviewed during the 1990 evaluation reported constraints in finance as the major limiting factor in construction of brick houses and the installation of good sanitation. They pointed out that while it was relatively easy for them to procure loans for items of equipment to enhance productivity, banks were reluctant to extend a similar line of credit for social improvements for the labour force. AFC loans, for example, could not be used for this type of investment. As for community mobilisation, FHWs claimed that it was difficult to motivate farm workers and their families to become involved in the actual work of digging, moulding bricks and construction. This was primarily because they felt that they were investing time and energy in something which would be lost to them if they left their jobs, and the probability that on the next farm they would have to do it all over again.

The situation of 'non-permanent' workers has also continued to give concern. The quality of their housing, the level of their wages, the health of their families, the education of their children, their levels of literacy continue to lag behind those of permanent workers. The 1991 national survey confirmed this increasing separation of the community into two camps, with conditions for one showing significant improvements in contrast to the other. Of permanent workers, some 45 per cent had brick houses, while less than 20 per cent of so called 'seasonal' workers had a similar facility. The trend to increase this percentage of the labour force against those with permanent status has also continued as farmers seek to avoid the protective legislation and its attendant costs introduced by the government in 1985. The large numbers of part-time, insecure, mobile workers has imposed constraints on the FHW programme in relation to community participation in health improvements on the farm. A survey of the FHW programme in Manicaland, eastern Zimbabwe, noted this difficulty:

Interviews with health workers in farming areas indicated that non-permanent labour were more difficult to reach and involve in primary health care. In one district in the Eastern province of Zimbabwe non-permanent households had less coverage by immunization, less FHW visits, less ante-natal care attendances, less outpatient curative visits and poorer participation in child spacing activities than permanent worker households. Clinic staff reported frustration in communicating with temporary workers who lacked continuity of contact with services.[1]

Unfortunately, without the power to enact more protective legislation in relation to working hours and conditions of employment, health promotion on the farms has also been undermined by unscrupulous labour practice.

A contract worker describes one common tactic for using labour to sustain profits, despite the attempts by the State to increase wages. This is the piece wage. Last year his 'mugwazo', or piece task, took him eight hours to complete. This year the task takes him about 14 hours to complete. As the piece work task increases, workers can spend up to 3 days on a single task, but only be paid a day's wages. Together with the effects of months of unemployment, the contract wage therefore, averages at less than a third of calculated subsistence needs.

(*Moto Magazine* 1986, p8)

The rise in piece work has largely fallen on the shoulders of women. Farmers are increasingly using their labour to avoid the expense of hiring workers from elsewhere during peak periods of need. The 1990 survey in Mashonaland Central indicated a doubling in the number of households with non-permanent female labour over a ten-year period. Despite the realisation of a higher family income there have been negative health consequences. Time taken to attend immunisation clinics, health promotion activities or to seek medical attention is time unpaid. During peak labour periods, therefore, FHW programmes have experienced reductions in women's attendance during mobile clinic visits. At the same time, after a day's work in the farmer's fields, there is still water, fuel and

---

1   Ministry of Health, 1987. 'An evaluation of the implementation of the Chipinge district health team plan in rural council areas', Ministry of Health, Harare.

Educational provision for farmworkers' children can be poor: A primary school on a commercial farm in Mashonaland West province.

food to be collected. The resulting strain on mothers has undermined childcare and other domestic chores.

Children are also caught up in the contract system. The 1990 Mashonaland survey on commercial farms estimated that 10 per cent of children over the age of five were used as labour. Schools were regularly emptied during planting, weeding and harvesting times, compromising the education of pupils. Very often, children were not paid by the farmer on the grounds that access to his school was sufficient remuneration. Yet again, a weakness in the labour laws has allowed this to continue. The Labour Relations Act of 1985 does not specifically prohibit the employment of children, only their forced exploitation. But with the almost complete dependence of families on the farm owner for their livelihood it is unlikely that they will refuse such a demand by the farmer, and risk eviction.

Farmworkers themselves readily acknowledge that they have acquiesced in the employment of their children, and on occasion asked employers to use them. Their inability to live on farm incomes, particularly those of non-permanent workers, is the main contributory cause. Figures for Mashonaland Central farms for 1989 indicated that even the permanent worker's salary of Z$134 per month stood at 54 per cent of the poverty datum line for an average family. It is clear that unless wage levels in this sector meet the minimum subsistence requirements of families, the use of female and child labour, and its attendant negative consequences on health and education, will continue.

Inadequate education facilities on many commercial estates has also confronted the health programme. Rebecca Goma confirmed that high levels of illiteracy undermine health promotion, affect attendance of families at clinics on specific dates and lead to misuse of prescriptions. Occupational health is similarly compromised due to the inability of workers to read the warnings on dangerous machinery or guides to safe usage of chemical pesticides and herbicides. Although numbers of pre-schools have substantially increased during the time of the FHW programme, large numbers of children receive no provision in relation to services thereafter. The number of farms with primary schools rose from 32 per cent to 47 per cent in a three-year period covered by the 1990 survey but it was also noted that 75 per cent of these establishments were unregistered as they failed to meet Ministry of Education standards. This means that they lack access to qualified teachers, educational materials and support from school inspectors and remedial education services. Many children on commercial farms have also missed out on Ministry of Education health promotion programmes such as the recent campaign on AIDS awareness in schools.

Provision of secondary-level education is even worse and, with only a few schools sited in commercial farming areas, most children do not progress beyond primary level. Those that do, often have to walk long distances to the nearest facility. One pupil in Centenary district claimed that by the time he had walked the 12km to school in the morning he was too tired to concentrate on his lessons. This lack of educational provision has created a cycle whereby children of farmworkers end up in the same situation as their parents, deprived of skills that might encourage them to move elsewhere. Lamented one worker on Dendere farm:

My father and mother were children of farm labourers. My brothers have ended up on farms. My sisters have married there too. Our children are poorly educated. What choice have they to do anything different from us? We would want them to move elsewhere but there is nothing for them but the same life as ourselves.

Whereas the FHW programme has been able to address in some measure the issue of environmental health through promotion of better sanitation, nutrition and hygiene, its success in the world of work has been more problematic. This seems partly to stem from the fact that many farmers will not countenance activities which could jeopardise profit margins through requiring substantial investment in the labour force in terms of industrial training, provision of adequate protective clothing and non-use of hazardous substances. Nor have sufficient linkages been established or commitments solicited from the Ministry of Labour which has the power to enact protective legislation and codes of practice in order to guarantee occupational safety.

Meanwhile the rise in capital investment in farm machinery, such as the doubling of the number of combine harvesters from 1980 to 1990, the increasing use of chemical pesticides, herbicides and fertiliser (estimated at a 300 per cent

Use of toxic herbicides and pesticides have caused health problems among farmworker communities. In a Ministry of Health survey in 1991, 50 per cent of farms where chemical spraying was carried out offered no protective clothing to the workers. Defective masks and sprays and unprotected storage facilities have also increased the risk of exposure to hazardous substances.

increase from 1980 to 1986), has brought with it high levels of occupational injury. In the 1990 Mashonaland Central survey, it was noted that one in ten households suffered an occupational injury in the previous year. This was reckoned to be an underestimate due to the non-recognition of many forms of occupational disease such as skin and lung conditions caused by contact with dangerous chemicals and tobacco dust.

Among the families who indicated an injury to a household member, none of those interviewed acknowledged compensation from either the farmer or the workers compensation fund (administered by the Ministry of Labour), even though some workers had been disabled. Ignorance about claim procedures and reluctance among farmers to accept financial responsibility for accidents were cited as reasons for the lack of redress to workers. The extent of risk to chemical exposure was further highlighted in the subsequent nationwide survey by the Ministry of Health in 1991, which established that up to 10 per cent of the workforce on farms was routinely involved in chemical spraying. Yet protective clothing was supplied in only little over half of the farms surveyed.

Ministry of Labour figures have consistently shown that agricultural workers experience higher rates of occupational injury than those in any other sector of the economy. Yet they continue to be the least monitored by safety inspectors, most of whose activities are concentrated on factories in urban areas. Lack of transport and resources to supervise farms, the fact that estates are not covered under the Factories and Works Act which stipulates minimum standards of safety, and a lack of political will to confront farmers on this issue have meant lack of

Joseph Phiri has worked on the farms of Mashonaland Central since 1948. In the early 1980s he began to lose sight in both eyes and now has very little vision left. Although the doctors he visited told him that the loss of his sight was probably caused by exposure to chemicals from the crop-spraying he used to carry out, he has had no luck when pressing his claim for compensation. The Workers Compensation Fund has indicated that, since no one employer is to blame, there is nothing they can do for him. Now living in a compound near Centenary, Joseph survives through the wages of his wife, employed as a part-time labourer on the farm. The partial loss of his sight, he was told by one former employer he approached for assistance, was his own responsibility.

protection for workers in the face of ever-greater occupational hazards.

Although the FHW programme has raised this issue with employers through representations by the workers' committees there is much that still remains to be achieved. Farm owners regularly blame the labour force for not wearing protective clothing issued to them, but the workers point out that the heavy-duty plastic garments and gumboots sometimes provided are unsuitable in the hot conditions under which they are expected to spray crops. Leaking barrels of chemicals, sprayers which drip contents onto workers and unprotected areas for mixing pesticides have caused acute and chronic poisoning, allergies and dermatitis, according to a survey on the use of organophosphates in the large-scale farming sector.[2]

Another trend is the increasing use of seasonal labour for this type of work, as permanent employees are granted preferential jobs as foremen, tractor drivers and work supervisors. Lack of job security has prevented seasonal workers from complaining about safety infringements for fear of dismissal. Furthermore, compensation for this category of worker is problematic. The consequences of exposure to hazardous substances can take a long time to develop into presentable symptoms, by which time a worker may have gone through several different employers, none of whom is willing to accept liability.

In a programme as widespread and diverse as that of the FHW scheme it is

---

2 Bwititi, T et al, 1987. 'Health hazards of organophosphate use among farmworkers in the large scale farming sector', *Central African Journal of Medicine* (May), pp120–126.

difficult to assess the overall willingness of farmers to go along with it or to oppose it. Yet in the more established programmes of Mashonaland Central, the evidence seems to show that farmers do welcome the presence of FHWs on their compounds. In the 1990 evaluation it was noted that within the project areas of Mvurwi, Mazoe and Bindura, almost all farms had one or two active FHWs. At the same time, 43 per cent of these had made a clinic facility available on the farm in 1989, compared with only 7 per cent before the programme began.

There was also a general consensus among farmers that the scheme was beneficial to all parties concerned. The most-acknowledged benefits included better hygiene, cleanliness of compounds and improved sanitation, availability of treatment for minor ailments, better childcare and pre-schools, and family planning. Farmer's wives also acknowledged that the FHW scheme had changed their roles from 'backdoor medics' to assistants in the social activities of the women, in particular support of income-generating projects, a change that was welcomed. The farm owners in Dendere and Tsoro also felt that the scheme had improved the relationship with the community and produced a better spirit and more unity among the workers themselves.

Yet while farmers may be willing to host the FHW scheme, the types of activity it can engage in are sometimes curtailed. Distributing information concerning labour rights, promoting safety regulations to protect the workforce and helping to strengthen the bargaining power and accountability of the workers committees are areas to which some farmers have objected. Therefore these measures have proved difficult to carry out. Problems also arise when the programme tries to confront the sustainability of its health initiatives and seeks a greater financial contribution from the farm owner. In a 1992 meeting in Mashonaland West province, for example, the question of a health levy from farmers to support the running of the programme was raised with them. While some supported the idea others were unhappy at the suggestion, declaring that they were already paying too much in rates and taxes and that health care was a government responsibility (Auret 1992). Conflicting levels of farmer commitment, therefore, have continued to plague the issue of FHW remuneration.

The 1991 national survey indicated that, although six out of ten FHWs were paid by the farmer, there was a wide range in the amount of the allowance paid. In the Marondera district of Mashonaland East, for example, the majority of FHWs in 1990 received little more than half of an average part-time wage that could be realised from farm work. Low levels of payment continue to be cited by FHWs as reasons for their departure from the programme. Of the 1,074 FHWs trained nationally between 1990 and 1992, 157 formally dropped out. The remainder, it should be noted, is not the actual number functioning effectively since many continue to supplement their meagre incomes from health promotion by engaging in part-time labour on their respective farms.

While the announcement of a national programme in 1990 was welcomed with enthusiasm by many participants in the various FHW schemes, difficulties have also hampered its development. In the area of training, limited funds have prevented adequate follow-up courses for FHWs who do require regular upgrading of skills. A review carried out by SIDA in 1993 (Auret 1992) also indicated that shortages of relevant teaching materials, qualified tutors and resources compromised the quality of tuition. In particular, trainers were felt to lack skills in participative teaching methodologies, preferring a lecture-style format that was inappropriate when replicated by FHWs in their respective communities. In addition supplies of medicines and support and supervision from mobile teams were erratic in many provinces.

The establishment of a national programme also failed to live up to the expectations of increased support and inter-ministerial cooperation that greeted its announcement. Part of the problem has been that the Ministry of Health has not created another tier of officers at the level of provincial and district hospitals to oversee the scheme adequately. The FHW programme has been added on to an already heavy workload and officers have complained of their inability to allocate sufficient time for coordination and programme development due to other commitments.

Whereas the provincial programme in Mashonaland Central formed a coordinating committee composed of not only health workers but also education officers, NGO representatives, trade union organisers, farm owners, agricultural extension workers, community development mobilisers, and so on, this breadth of representation is still lacking at national level. A truly inter-ministerial team reflecting the commitment of government to a multi-sectoral approach to the problem of farmworkers remains to be realised. Yet, as the Mashonaland Central example seems to indicate, unless these other services are included, health programmes are limited in what they can achieve.

7
Looking to the future

If need constitutes one of the criteria for development assistance, then farmworker communities in Zimbabwe are certainly a major priority. The statistics are there for all to read: the worst rates of malnutrition, maternal mortality and communicable disease, the poorest accommodation and sanitation provision, the lowest levels of health care, education and social services in the country. The physical evidence is also incontrovertible. No one visiting a cramped compound on the tobacco farms of Mashonaland province or the agro-industrial estates of eastern Zimbabwe can fail to be moved by the squalor and plight of its inhabitants, the desperation of its older people and migrant workers as they approach their declining years, the hopelessness of young people faced with lives as unpromising as those of their parents.

Yet, as poverty and need increase, the more difficult it often seems for development to take place. Contrast community participation, for example, in the commercial farms and those of the neighbouring communal areas where much of the successful health interventions since independence have been realised through local initiative. In the former, lack of job security and property rights, lower levels of education, years of social neglect and exploitation have created communities often unwilling to change the situation from which they might be evicted at any time.

The structural factors behind this poverty can also seem immovable. There is the entrenchment of the commercial farming system in the political and economic life of Zimbabwe. The authority of private property owners overshadows and limits the type of activity that is needed to improve the health and welfare of their workers. There is the legal system too, which should protect the weak and deprived in any society, yet which in Zimbabwe has sufficient loopholes to allow farm owners to continue to ignore workers' rights in relation to occupational safety, job security and rates of pay. Faced with these kinds of difficulties it is little wonder, perhaps, that the majority of international NGOs involved in rural development have concentrated their assistance in the communal areas of the country. This is not to dispute the very real needs of these other communities but it has meant that a considerable proportion of the nation's population has continued to go without.

Yet despite the difficulties facing it, the FHW scheme has displayed considerable tenacity and imagination in trying to find ways to improve conditions for farm labour. One of the lessons it has to offer development workers is the value of patience. As mentioned in Chapter 4, a typical timescale of NGO assistance, the standard two-to-three-year project commitment, is inadequate if part of the goal is to awaken community initiative and the real participation of its beneficiaries. One need solved awakens other demands and it is important that project initiators help sustain the process and do not abandon communities once that first step has been taken.

The example of Dendere farm is instructive. Discussion as to the causes of poor health in families gave rise to a desire to supplement family incomes. This occasioned the initiation of income-generating projects which required support in terms of start-up capital and training in book-keeping, accounts and management. These projects in turn were accompanied by a demand for literacy which also necessitated programme support. Is it too much to expect that in time a more literate population will begin to demand other rights such as education for their children and the right to vote in local elections or achieve the unity and cohesion collectively to challenge the poverty of their circumstances?

The development of the FHW programme also outlines the importance of not allowing a project plan to run ahead of community capacity to understand and assimilate it. If part of the aim of participatory development is that the community comes in some measure to own the project rather than simply passively receiving another service, then time taken to work through local structures that inspire respect is crucial. The mobilisation and development of workers' committees, traditional healers and birth attendants, the farm foreman and women's groups has taken considerable time, yet without it the acceptance of health initiatives on compounds and the FHW within the community would have been much more problematic.

At the same time, this priority has involved some reorientation of skills among health workers, both local and international, who visited the farming areas to initiate and supervise the programme. In particular they have had to learn the value of listening, something which can be difficult when faced with an illiterate, dependent and sometimes unmotivated workforce. A nurse with the mobile clinic that services the commercial farming areas around Centenary put it in these words:

As professional nurses we have been taught to inform and instruct rather than listen. But since the aim of the programme was to involve farm workers in meeting their own health needs we realised that this approach was wrong. We had to look at other ways of working with the people and listen to their priorities rather than insist on our own.

The FHW programme also displays the value of flexibility. Given the fact that, for the reasons outlined in Chapter 3, the state was unable or unwilling to insist on a comprehensive strategy to alleviate the plight of farmworkers after 1980, or allocate the kind of resources that would have meant significant changes to their living environment, this kind of approach was possibly the only one that could succeed. The programme operated on private property, always subject to the whims and wishes of the farm owner who could effectively block any initiatives if he so desired. Rural council antagonism could also have sabotaged development efforts on farms. In the absence of any other local government structure, they also offered a possibility of some longer-term administrative continuity for the project. Much of the effort of the programme was therefore spent on trying to win these over to the side of development on behalf of the farmworkers, despite their previous reluctance to do so. This required considerable skills of diplomacy and non-confrontation at a time in Zimbabwean history when farmers were suspicious and distrustful of any 'interference' in the affairs of their workers.

The programme also needed the contributions of a range of institutions and people with competing interests who had never worked together. Potential antagonists, such as commercial farmers on the one hand and trade union organisers on the other, Ministry of Health personnel and rural council officials, farm health workers and the foremen and employers with whom they had to deal were asked to abandon the suspicion and distrust that had sometimes characterised their previous relations, in order to work together for the benefit of the farmworker community. Perhaps one of the most valuable lessons that the FHW scheme can offer us is that of compromise, the importance of working through what is there rather than dreaming of what might have been different.

Chapters 4 and 5 have discussed some of the concrete achievements that have been realised as a result of such efforts but perhaps the major change is more subtle and invisible. Farm labourers and their families in the past saw health as a privilege rather than a basic right they could demand from society. The farm health workers programme has come into their compounds and informed them that this is not the case, that through a combination of their own efforts and outside assistance they need not live in perpetual fear of becoming ill. Community perceptions in some of the more established project areas seem to have changed, judging by the developments in areas that workers themselves can influence. According to a trade union officer in Bindura, this has been accompanied by a new confidence on some of these compounds, a new spirit of questioning:

> *Workers are now asking why there is no clinic for miles around. Why do people in towns have several hospitals and numerous doctors? Why do they lose a day's wages when collecting medicine for a sick child? Why are they evicted from farms where they have spent their lives contributing to the wealth of others?*

Yet while this type of questioning is a credit to the community mobilisation aspects of the programme it also poses a very different type of challenge to its further development. As workers come more and more to understand the causes behind their ill health – the lack of legal protection, poor wages, inadequate education, insecurity of tenure, and so on – new demands may be placed on project partners to assist in other types of activity and support. This might involve a greater need for advocacy work to raise the profile of the farmworker community within the country so that the more structural causes behind their poor health also begin to be challenged.

There is the problem of 'seasonal' workers and the legal inadequacies that have permitted their exploitation by unscrupulous employers. There needs to be a campaign against the 'piece-wage' system on grounds of its inherent unfairness as well as its detrimental effects on the health of farmworker families. There needs to be an end to the exploitative use of children, not only to protect their health and educational interests but to prevent farmers from using a cheap alternative to hiring permanent adult workers. The increasing risk of occupational injury in the wake of new trends in mechanisation and chemical usage also needs to be tackled. At the level of the workforce, training in occupational safety should form a compulsory part of the conditions of service. Workers also need to be informed of their labour rights in relation to use of machinery and hazardous substances, backed up by improved state regulation to prevent employers from exposing them to unnecessary dangers. In the event of injury a speedier and more simple system of compensation also needs to be enacted.

Healthy, secure and well-housed workers are as much of a productive investment as items of machinery. Financial institutions should extend a borrowing facility to commercial farmers for environmental improvements. This should be backed up by minimum standards legislation for social conditions on farm compounds. Educational facilities also need to be increased to levels comparable with those in other parts of the country. The invisibility of farmworkers needs to be addressed, in particular their lack of voice in local government. The new programme to amalgamate rural and district councils has not dealt with the disenfranchisement of farmworkers. Indeed there are worries that farm labour will not only have to compete against farm owners for access to resources but also against the communal inhabitants now included under the umbrella of the joint council. Since both of these groups have representation through their respective elected candidates, farmworkers may now come third rather than second when the financial vote is divided.

This book began with a description of the colonial seizure of land and how the eviction of the indigenous population from prime agricultural areas of the country lay at the heart of the inequalities between white and black, rich and poor in pre-independence Zimbabwe. Perhaps it is appropriate, therefore, to end with the centrality of these events to the welfare of farmworkers, and why the issue of land rights for them also needs to be raised. Land redistribution was one of the major rallying cries of the liberation struggle. As Chapter 3 outlined, however, a set of economic, political and legal constraints prevented the new government from addressing this fundamental imbalance in Zimbabwean society. Yet, 15 years after independence the patience of the African rural population is wearing thin. Commercial farm land has been seized by communal farmers. government officials are regularly harangued during their visits to communal areas about the overcrowding, unemployment, soil erosion and food shortages that are reaching unbearable proportions.

In response to these pressures and in honour of its prior commitment the government announced in 1993 a new policy of land redistribution. Under this programme some 5 million hectares of underutilised commercial farm land are to be targeted for eventual resettlement by communal farmers who, it is hoped, will receive sufficient training and financial support to maintain high levels of productivity.[1] Yet up to the time of publication, government plans had not mentioned farmworkers and their families already resident in those areas, for whom land is just as important. Envisaged criteria of eligibility for the programme, such as ownership of five head of cattle, exclude them from consideration. In some ways their needs are greater than those of communal inhabitants who, despite the problems outlined above, at least retain land use rights in their home areas unlike many farmworkers of migrant descent.

Any programme of assistance to commercial farmworkers needs to address this issue of their long-term security. It is a factor that they constantly raise themselves as an impediment to change. Faced with the prospect of an uncertain and probably impoverished old age, the scope of their participation and commitment to health and other environmental improvements on their compounds is limited. Farm workers, therefore, need to be involved in the land redistribution exercise so that they too have access to the resource that can guarantee them most stability. Land also needs to be designated as residential areas for those farmworkers who are too old to develop their own property, and supported with inputs such as water, housing, electricity and other social services. Without such a permanent stake in their environment it is unrealistic to expect individuals to come together and function effectively as a coherent and stable community. A secure future is essential in strengthening the confidence of farmworkers to challenge all the factors described in this book that negatively affect their lives.

---

1   In an assessment of land use in LSF areas in 1986, researchers found that the most intensively cultivated districts of Mashonaland produced crops only on slightly over half the available hectarage, despite being in the most-favoured land areas. The authors concluded that two-thirds to one-half of Zimbabwe's prime agricultural land was neither cropped nor fallowed. (Weiner, D et al, 1986. 'Land and agricultural productivity in Zimbabwe', *Journal of African Studies*, Vol 23, pp251–285.)

Bibliography

Auret, D, 1992. 'A review of the farm health worker programme from 1990–92', Swedish International Development Agency.

Bratton, M, 1981. 'Development in Zimbabwe – strategy and tactics', *Journal of Modern African Studies*.

Chisvo, Munhamo, 1992. *Some indicators of the impact of adjustment on social services in Zimbabwe*, UNICEF – Zimbabwe.

Davies, W, 1990. *We cry for our land – farm workers in South Africa*, Oxfam, Oxford.

Duncan, B, 1973. 'The wages and labour supply position in European agriculture', *Rhodesian Journal of Economics*, Vol 7, pp1–13.

Hanlon, 1986. *Beggar your neighbours – apartheid power in Southern Africa*, CIIR, London.

Herbst, J, 1990. *State politics in Zimbabwe*, University of Zimbabwe, Harare.

Jensen, S, 1992. 'Our forefathers' blood', MS Dokumentation, published by Mellemfolkeligt Samvirke.

Loewenson, R, 1990. 'Evaluation of health in large scale farming areas – 1990', Save The Children Fund (UK), London.

Loewenson, R, 1992. *Modern plantation agriculture*, Zed Books, London.

Loewenson and Chinhori, 1986. 'The socio-economic situation of commercial farm workers in Zimbabwe', SIDA review.

Loewenson, R, Zanza, J and Mushayandebvu, I, 1983. 'An interim evaluation of the Bindura Farm Health Worker Project', SCF(UK), Harare (mimeo).

Mandaza, et al, 1986. *Zimbabwe: the political economy of transition, 1980–1986*, CODESRIA Books, Dakar.

Ministry of Health, 1987. *Maternal and Child Health Annual Report*, MoH, Harare.

Riddell, R, 1980. 'Zimbabwe: A New Nation With Old Problems', *Institute of Development Studies Bulletin*, Vol II, No 4, IDS, Sussex.

Rifkind, ML, 1968. 'The politics of land in Rhodesia', University of Edinburgh, MSc thesis.

Roussos, P, 1988. *Zimbabwe – an introduction to the economics of transformation*, Baobab Books, Harare.

Sayce, et al, 1987. 'Tabex encyclopedia Zimbabwe', Quest, Harare.

Schmidt, E, 1992. *Peasants, traders and wives*, Baobab Books, Harare.

Selous, FC, 1893. *Travel and adventure in South-East Africa*, Century Publishing, London.

Stoneman, et al, 1981. *Zimbabwe's inheritance*, Macmillan, Basingstoke.

Thompson, C, 1991. *Harvests Under Fire*, Zed Books, London.

UNDP, 1980. *Zimbabwe – towards a new order: an economic and social survey*, United Nations.

Warndorff, T, 1990. 'Evaluation of a two years farm health programme', Save The Children Fund (UK), London.

World Bank, 1983. *Accelerated development in sub-Saharan Africa: an agenda for action*.

QUEEN ELIZABETH HOUSE LIBRARY

Catholic Institute for International Relations

CIIR works to overcome poverty and injustice in the Third World. Founded in 1940, it is an independent charity which works with people of any religious belief or none.

Tackling the issues

CIIR's **Education Programme** provides information on socio-economic, political, human rights and church issues in the Third World. It has sections working on Asia, Latin America and Southern Africa, and one which analyses the international causes of Third World poverty.

Sharing Skills

International Cooperation for Development, CIIR's overseas programme, recruits a wide range of experienced professionals to share their skills in small-scale development projects in Latin America, the Caribbean, Southern Africa and the Middle East.

If you would like to know more about CIIR, or if you would like to join CIIR, please contact:

Membership Secretary, CIIR, Unit 3, Canonbury Yard,
190a New North Road, London N1 7BJ, UK.
Tel 0171 354 0883. Fax 0171 359 0017.

Membership: UK £15, unwaged £5, Overseas £20.

CIIR members receive *CIIR News* four times a year, CIIR's *Annual Review*, and a range of pamphlets, including titles in the *Comment* series. Members are offered special discounts on CIIR publications.

KU-309-304

756
'GAL

IEA Health Unit Paper No. 7

COMPETING FOR THE DISABLED

WITHDRAWN

WITHDRAWN

WITHDRAWN

Competing for the Disabled

Charles S.B. Galasko and Caroline Lipkin

Introduction

by

Ian McColl

WITHDRAWN

London
The IEA Health Unit
1989

First published in September 1989
by
The IEA Health Unit
2 Lord North St
London SW1P 3LB

© The IEA Health Unit 1989

All rights reserved

ISBN 0-255 36256-0

Typeset by the IEA Health Unit
Printed in Great Britain by
Goron Pro-Print Co. Ltd
Churchill Industrial Estate, Lancing, West Sussex

v

Contents

Foreword

Government provision of health care is usually justified as a means of ensuring that the most vulnerable people receive the best quality care. However, the reality for some 40 years has been that the NHS and related official agencies have offered an inferior service to the disabled, particularly wheelchair users and patients who require artificial limbs and appliances.

Competing for the Disabled has been written jointly by Professor Charles Galasko, a consultant orthopaedic surgeon from the Hope Hospital in Manchester, and Caroline Lipkin of the IEA Health Unit. The general message of their study is that current public provision for users of wheelchairs and artificial limbs and appliances is inadequate. Indeed, government, in the form of the NHS, the Department of Health and the Artificial Limb and Appliance Centres, has served as a straitjacket impeding consumer choice and preventing the private sector from performing at its best. It does so, *inter alia*, because the government imposes detailed design specifications on the private sector. Standard NHS wheelchairs, for instance, are made only for the NHS and no company offers a product of such low quality on the open market.

There is a proper role for government in making available wheelchairs and artificial limbs, but a different public-private mix is called for. Instead of supplying goods in kind and telling manufacturers how to design products, government should confine itself to ensuring that all disabled people enjoy the purchasing power to obtain mobility aids. Forty years of supplying wheelchairs in kind and stipulating how they should be designed has produced a shabby and inferior service for some of the most vulnerable people in the land.

The superior alternative of giving people a measure of purchasing power, to enable them to choose from among different suppliers and make it possible for producers to offer the best that technology can provide, was the very solution recommended by an official inquiry into the supply of wheelchairs conducted under the chairmanship of Professor Ian McColl of Guy's Hospital. The McColl Report advocated a voucher scheme and, although most of its proposals were accepted by the government, this pivotal recommendation to create consumer choice through vouchers was rejected. Professor, now Lord, McColl has written an introduction to *Competing for the Disabled* and reviews developments since his report was published. He gives credit where it is due but pulls no punches in his criticism of remaining government failures. Reform to permit greater competition and consumer sovereignty is now long overdue.

Finally, I am grateful to Sir Reginald Murley, a member of our Advisory Council, for suggesting this project and for his comments on early drafts. I am also grateful to the following for their comments: Professor Robert Pinker, Rachel Hurst of the Greenwich Association of Disabled People's Centre for Independent Living, Mike Solly and Lord Harris.

David G. Green
July 1989

Introduction

Ian McColl

The Author

Professor Lord McColl of Dulwich, MS, FRCS, FACS, is Director of Surgery at Guy's Hospital. He was educated at Hutchesons' Grammar School, Glasgow, and St Paul's School, London, where he won scholarships in classics. He is a member of the Council of the Royal College of Surgeons, and President of the Mildmay Mission Hospital. Following his Chairmanship of a Government Working Party on the supply of artificial limbs and wheelchairs in England he was made Vice-Chairman of the Disablement Services Authority.

Introduction

Government disquiet about the quality of the service given to amputees and wheelchair users led to the establishment of a working party to review the adequacy, quality and management of the various services received by patients in the Artificial Limb and Appliance Centres (ALACs) in England, and on the respective roles of the staff of the Centres, the NHS and manufacturers. The Working Party was asked to look at ways of promoting efficiency and cost effectiveness, but there was no question of cutting the £80m budget. The McColl Report was presented in 1986 and revealed a can of worms, a service which was poor in many ways due to inadequate management and virtually no competition between contractors.

The Government accepted almost all the recommendations of the report and set up a special health authority, called the Disablement Services Authority (DSA), in July 1987 charged with putting the service right and then integrating it with the National Health Service in 1991. This is the first special health authority to be run by a mixture of civil servants (mostly from the DHSS) and officers seconded from the NHS. The members of the Authority come from many walks of life and include an occupational therapist, an ex-vice chancellor confined to a wheelchair, a distinguished former Government minister also severely disabled, the chairman of a regional health authority, a district health authority manager, two businessmen with extensive commercial experience, and a Professor of Surgery.

Poor Management

The major defect in the old ALAC system was poor management. This is being tackled by a new structure of specially recruited regional management. Each DSA region corresponds to its regional health authority and liaison is proceeding apace with the 1991 integration in view. The regional managers are responsible for running and improving the service and will have their own budgets for 1989-90. In the early days of the Working Party it was recognised that there was no effective financial control of the service. Much time and effort has been devoted to rectifying this. A working group of officials and Members of the DSA has started work on performance indicators which will accurately assess the quality of care in terms of the number of visits required to fit a comfortable limb, etc. Consultants have been employed to put proper financial systems in place, and a major accountancy firm has been retained to provide an internal audit service. The finance function itself is being contracted out, to secure a more comprehensive service at a lower cost than was possible in-house. The whole basis of accounting has been revised from a cash basis (which has to be maintained in parallel for Parliamentary Vote accounting purposes) to one of income and expenditure, which reveals the true level of consumption of resources.

Voucher Option

One of the great disappointments has been the failure to introduce the voucher principle for wheelchairs which was recommended by the McColl committee. The proposal was to give wheelchair users the option of an appropriate wheelchair from the Disablement Services Centre or a voucher equivalent to the value of the wheelchair plus the cost of the service. This would not only give the customer more choice but also stimulate the Disablement Services Centre staff to give a good service to compete for the customer. If too many customers opted for vouchers, the demand for the service would be reduced and their jobs be less secure. Those accepting a voucher would be able to add their own money in order to buy what they deemed to be a more acceptable chair. Such a system would have a bureaucratic cost, but it would also require primary legislation. The Authority has therefore decided not to pursue the proposal unless and until vouchers are introduced for other parts of the health services.

The Artificial Limb Service

The McColl Report reached the conclusion that limb-fitting services in England were inferior to those in some other Western countries and that this state of affairs could be improved in three ways. Firstly, by modernising the training of the prosthetists; secondly, encouraging them to leave the suffocating influence of the monopoly suppliers and set up independent prosthetic companies; and thirdly, to establish with the monopoly limb suppliers separate contracts for component supply and provision of prosthetic and repair services. An attempt to block the latter plan was made by two major suppliers (subsidiaries of the InterMed group, part of BTR), who took legal action to prevent the proposed separation of contracts without three years' notice. The Authority won the case with costs.

The artificial limb service (and subsequently the wheelchair service) was set up with the best of intentions to provide an excellent service first to limbless ex-servicemen and later to encompass the whole population. Eventually it served 65,000 amputees (and almost half a million wheelchair users). The Government, in the shape of the DHSS, was the monopsonist and BTR the monopolist supplying and fitting 75% of limbs in the UK. Such a tidy arrangement might have been expected to have given a good service to the customer. The commercial companies would know roughly every year what was demanded of them and this kind of stability should have led to a cost effective and efficient service. The reverse was the reality. The monopolists enjoyed cost-plus contracts for 40 years, and there was no effective control over the costs. There was a comfortable relationship between monopolist and monopsonist, sheltered from the cold winds of the market place.

This effectively precluded competitive prices and a decent service for disabled people. Involvement in the market-place by Government departments, however well inten-tioned, simply does not work. Human nature will always take advantage of any situation where sticks and carrots do not operate. At the end of the line the customer was ill-served and there was a lack of prompt delivery, courtesy and prosthetic skills. Clearly the close-knit suppliers' ring had to be opened up to competition and the prosthetist liberated from the oppressive employment of the monopoly in order to be free to use modern methods of fitting and give a much more personal service to the customer.

Last summer, a start was made to opening up the market by letting prosthetic service contracts to two firms, one of them a firm of independent prosthetists. Experience with them has shown artificial limbs being supplied to patients much more quickly, delivery times being measured in days rather than the weeks or months of the old regime.

More recently the Disablement Services Authority invited tenders separately for hardware and prosthetic services at all but three of its Centres. This tender round provoked considerable interest. Tenders for hardware were received from the major suppliers including a West German firm. Tenders for prosthetic services were received from eighteen companies, twelve of which were new to this field. Price and quality of service were the chief determinants in award-ing contracts which resulted in the previous InterMed monopoly being broken with a large number of new con-tractors entering the field. Even if InterMed wins all the remaining Centres, its share of the market would stand at around 15% compared with about 75% previously. The monopolist simply priced itself out of the market.

Training

As far as prosthetic training is concerned, the Authority is committed to improving the training of prosthetists and increasing their number. The problem is complicated by the disarray of orthotic services throughout the country, since prosthetic and orthotic education and training are closely linked. In order to solve both these problems the Authority is backing proposals for an integrated training of prosthetists and orthotists to degree level at Salford University. It is hoped that the number of trainees at Strathclyde University will be increased too. Hitherto, only employees of the limb contractors were admitted for prosthetic training. Discussions are under way to end this and to place the training on a proper student basis.

The services for which the Disablement Services Authority is responsible will form the core of a much improved rehabilitation service in the National Health Service. Frequent visits and consultations with all fourteen regions have been in progress to further this end and to prod the less responsive brethren into action.

Wheelchairs

One of the major problems facing the Authority is the lack of control over the prescription of wheelchairs. Most such prescription has up to now been by general practitioners, each of whom may encounter the task rarely. In effect, the Authority is like a giant store distributing goods to people who ask for them, most of whom are oblivious of the cost and are not aware of the intricacies. As a result, the volume of demand is enormous, with consequent delay in delivery, and many of those receiving chairs hardly use them. Meanwhile, the most severely disabled people, who are affected most by the delays, get chairs with which they are often dissatisfied. The Authority's policy of devolution of the wheelchair service to district level means that assessment in the future will be carried out in the main by therapists who have been specially trained for the job. They will eventually have budgetary responsibility too. The range of chairs available is being reviewed and revised, and a pilot study has begun for the supply to the most severely disabled of an occupant-controlled powered chair suitable for use both indoors and outdoors. This was an important recommendation of the McColl working party. The study will involve 200 chairs from three manufacturers, and will be carried out at Newcastle and Manchester. It will last a year and its principal objectives are to evaluate the real benefit of this type of chair to the users, to test criteria for prescription, and to assess the number of people who might qualify for such chairs. Both new wheelchair users and some more experienced ones will be given the opportunity to take part in this study which will be carefully evaluated.

Conclusions

Progress has been made in tackling the problems identified by the McColl Report, but moving through the thick bureaucratic and professional treacle is always difficult. It is true to say that both officials and Members of the Authority sometimes feel frustrated by the apparently slow rate of change. Nonetheless, the customer is beginning to see a friendlier face in the service, which now adheres to the principle that the customer is always right. Much remains to be done to produce more comfortable artificial limbs and wheelchairs without delay or hassle and to concentrate the available resources on those who really need them: there is no point in torturing elderly amputees with limbs they have no wish to wear.

Splashing largesse around is the lazy and easy way of solving the social conscience. Taking the trouble to find out who really needs help and then ensuring that they get it must be the real answer to these thorny problems.

London
July 1989

Ian McColl
Guy's Hospital

Competing for the Disabled

Charles S.B. Galasko

and

Caroline Lipkin

The Authors

Charles S.B. Galasko, MB,BCH,CHM,FRCS(Eng),FRCS(Ed) is Professor of Orthopaedic Surgery at the University of Manchester. He is Consultant Orthopaedic Surgeon to the Salford Health Authority and works at the Royal Manchester Children's Hospital and Hope Hospital. He has a particular interest in the physically handicapped and runs a Specialised Muscle Clinic, to which patients with a variety of neuromuscular disorders are referred from afar. Many of these patients require specialised wheelchairs, orthoses and prostheses. He is the author, or co-author and editor, of seven books and over 150 articles. His publications include *Neuromuscular Problems in Orthopaedics* (Blackwell Scientific Publications, 1987), *Skeletal Metastases* (Butterworths, 1986), and *Imaging Techniques in Orthopaedics* (Springer Verlag, 1989).

Caroline Lipkin is Research and Editorial Assistant in the Health Unit at the Institute of Economic Affairs, having been research assistant since 1987. Prior to joining the Health Unit she was a postgraduate student at the University of Bradford, where she received her master's degree in business administration. She was an undergraduate at the Hebrew University of Jerusalem, Israel, before gaining a batchelor's degree in social policy in 1986.

Introduction

Although there have been major developments during the past ten to fifteen years in the design of artificial limbs (prostheses), appliances (orthoses) such as calipers and trusses, and wheelchairs, patient dissatisfaction with the provision of these aids through the National Health Service and Artificial Limb and Appliance Centres is increasing. This is largely due to the delays in implementing new designs; delays in providing orthoses, prostheses and wheelchairs; and poor quality control resulting in poor fit when they are eventually provided. In May 1984 dissatisfaction with the Artificial Limb and Appliance Centre (ALAC) services led to the establishment of a working party under the chairmanship of Professor Ian McColl, professor of surgery at the United Medical Schools of Guy's and St Thomas' Hospitals, London, and director of surgery at Guy's Hospital.

The McColl Report[1] was published in January 1986 and this paper evaluates its contribution to improving ALAC. Chapter 1 describes the history of the artificial limb and wheelchair services and Chapters 2 and 3 discuss the McColl Report's findings, recommendations and implementation. Deficiencies in NHS services for disabled people, and in particular the orthotic service, are dealt with in Chapter 4. Chapter 5 considers the public provision of wheelchairs, artificial limbs and appliances in the USA. Chapter 6 summarises our recommendations for the further improvement of ALAC and NHS services for the physically disabled.

---

[1] *Review of Artificial Limb and Appliance Centre Services: The Report of an Independent Working Party Under the Chairmanship of Professor Ian McColl,* London: HMSO, 1986. Volume 1, *The Report;* Volume 2, *Annexes.*

1

A Brief History

The large number of soldiers who lost limbs during the First World War led to the foundation of a state artificial limb and wheelchair service. In 1915 the war office converted a mansion at Roehampton into a hospital for war pensioner amputees, and following Lord Kitchener's death in 1916, the Earl Kitchener Memorial Fund was formed to provide invalid chairs for disabled war pensioners. Responsibility for providing the service was given to the Ministry of Pensions, established in 1916. (In practice the Earl Kitchener Memorial Fund continued to provide the wheelchair service, from 1919 in conjunction with the Red Cross.) The Ministry of Pensions also provided other services including appliances and motor vehicles for war pensioners. In 1987 approximately 3,000 war pensioners were still using the ALAC service.

Responsibility for provision of ALAC services remained with the Ministry of Pensions until 1953 when it was passed to the Ministry of Health. By then the NHS had been created and the ALAC service was required to provide for all permanently disabled people regardless of whether or not their needs stemmed from war injuries. Civilians became entitled to 'free' wheelchairs and 30,000 or so amputees were made eligible for 'free' artificial limbs.

In 1968 the ALAC service passed to the DHSS where it remained until July 1987 when it was transferred to a special Disablement Services Authority (DSA). It is the task of the DSA to plan the transfer of ALAC to the NHS health authorities by 1 April 1991.

The position in other parts of the UK varied in some degree from the English model. In Wales the Welsh Office became responsible for the service until 1 April 1988 when it was transferred to the Welsh Health Common Services Authority. In Scotland the service was integrated into the NHS in 1953 immediately upon its transfer from the Ministry of Pensions.

Today the DSA provides for approximately 65,000 amputees, including 5,000 new ones each year, and more than a third of a million people who are loaned about 500,000 wheelchairs. The cost of the ALAC service was around £90 million in 1987-88.

Background

Since the mid-1950s ALAC has had to cope with considerable changes in both the nature and level of demand made on its services. No longer are its principal clients ex-servicemen; today most users of the service are elderly people. About 78 per cent of all lower limb amputations are for patients aged over 60, suffering diseases of the vascular system and half of all wheelchair users are over 70. The influx of the elderly into the service has heightened the demand for new services, especially cheaper light-weight artificial limbs and wheelchairs now possible because of developments in technology and materials. New limb systems incorporating modular techniques, which enable the greater part of the artificial limb to be put together on the spot from adaptable prefabricated components, giving improved mobility and lighter weight, are now available. And wheelchairs, especially powered ones, continue to become ever more sophisticated.

Partly as a result of these pressures the number of complaints about the service increased throughout the late 1970s and early 1980s. In particular the limb fitting and delivery services were criticised. Amputees were having to wait weeks, and often months for their limbs which when they eventually arrived did not fit properly.

In 1983 dissatisfaction with the ALAC service was officially recognised. The Minister for the Disabled, Sir Hugh

Rossi, announced the setting up of a working party to find out what was wrong with the service and put it right. Following the general election his successor, Tony Newton, established the working party under the chairmanship of Professor Ian McColl to investigate the service in England. It had the following terms of reference:

> to review and report on the adequacy, quality and management of the various services received by patients in Artificial Limb and Appliance Centres in England, and on the respective roles of the staff of the centres, the NHS and manufacturers, having regard to the need to promote efficiency and cost-effectiveness.[1]

The other members of the working party were: Sir Austin Bunch, president of the British Limbless Ex-Service Men's Association; Elizabeth Fanshawe, director of the Disabled Living Foundation; Professor Brian Griffiths, head of the Policy Unit at 10 Downing Street; Mr M J Hussey,chairman of the BBC; Mr Peter Janes, marketing director of Gillette UK Limited; and Dr C B Wynn-Parry, consultant advisor in rehabilitation to the DHSS.

---

[1] *Report*, Vol. 1, p. 1.

2

The McColl Report

The Working Party's report ('The McColl Report') was published in January 1986. It is a fiercely critical review of the finance and workings of the ALAC service. At the time of the investigation the service comprised 30 ALACs run by the DHSS, separately from the NHS, through headquarters in Blackpool, Roehampton and Russell Square, London, employing 38 full-time doctors and over 1,000 administrative, technical and clerical staff.

Artificial limbs are supplied by commercial firms who work under contract to the DHSS. There are three major and two minor lower limb contractors and one upper limb contractor. The two largest companies, Hanger and Vessa, are both owned by the InterMed Group which supplies over 70 per cent of lower limbs in the UK. The limb companies employ some 200 prosthetists whose job is to fit the artificial limb to the patient. Fitting takes place at the patient's nearest ALAC, but a significant amount of manufacturing is carried out in central workshops and factories.

Wheelchairs are bought in and delivered to users from central stores or direct from manufacturers. In contrast to the artificial limb industry there are a large number of wheelchair firms and repair services are separated. Once supplied, chairs are maintained by a network of local 'approved repairers'. A substantial private sector exists and many disabled people have preferred to buy wheelchairs at their own expense.

The McColl report makes 49 detailed recommendations based above all on the belief that competition and choice are required to improve the quality and efficiency of ALAC services. This paper is mainly concerned with McColl's proposals for the artificial limb and wheelchair service.

ALAC involvement in the provision of invalid vehicles has steadily declined since the introduction of Mobility Allowance in 1976 as the main form of help with long-range mobility. It is our belief that if the McColl recommendations are implemented in spirit as well as in name, a far more consumer orientated and efficient service will emerge.

Organisation, management and medical services

McColl believed that the ALAC services lacked a clearly defined management function:

> Many of the failings we have seen arise quite simply because no one executive is in charge. In fact, there are no executives about — there are administrators, technical staff and doctors, described by one senior official as 'a driverless troika', and this has led to a lack of accountability and no clear lines of overall responsibility.[1]

The effects of poor management were made worse by the fact that:

> Senior officials came and went from their ALAC posts with depressing regularity and frequency. No one stayed long enough to carry through improvements, to be accountable for changes initiated or even to plan what was necessary.

Moreover, senior officials brought to the service

> little by way of management skills or experience relevant to running a multi-disciplinary commercial type organisation.[2]

---

[1] *Report,* Vol. 1, para. 144.

[2] *Op. cit., para. 145.*

A new independent organisation, headed by a management board, served by a chief executive and answerable to the Minister of the Disabled, was recommended by McColl to manage ALAC services. And in keeping with the commercial nature of ALAC, management was to be strictly on business lines.[1]

The working party felt it to be of vital importance that the new organisation should be separately funded:

> There was virtual unanimity amongst all those submitting evidence to us that the ALAC budget should continue to be separately protected as now...we believe that it is imperative...to fund the services separately as at present.[2]

Protected funding would lessen the risks of ALAC becoming a 'cinderella' service which would be the likely outcome if ALAC had to compete for monies against other medical specialties.

At local level McColl recommended that each ALAC should be headed by a clinical director who has appropriate recognised training in rehabilitation medicine and who is conversant with prosthetics and orthotics. He would have responsibility for co-ordinating the full rehabilitation of his ALAC clients.[3] It was emphasised that existing ALAC doctors could not automatically be made clinical directors. They would need to fulfil the Royal College of Physicians', (RCP) criteria for training in rehabilitation medicine before being considered.

---

[1] *ibid.*

[2] *Report,* Vol. 1, para. 148.

[3] *Op. cit.,* para. 20.

The proposal for a clinical director was echoed by the RCP.[1] However they recommend the incorporation of ALACs into new NHS regional disability units headed by consultants in disability medicine.

The Artificial Limb Service

At the time of the McColl Report the service provided for about 63,000 patients, over 50,000 of whom were lower limb amputees. Limbs were supplied through 18 main ALACs and 9 subcentres. The DHSS was responsible for administering the service but commercial firms under contract to the Department were responsible for the supply, fitting and maintenance of the limbs. There were three major suppliers of lower limbs, J.E. Hanger and Co. Ltd, Vessa Ltd and Chas A Blatchford and Sons Ltd, plus two smaller ones. Hugh Steeper Ltd was the only upper limb contractor.

The total UK market for lower limbs and associated prosthetic services amounted to about £35 million in 1987. Of this, 52 per cent was accounted for by new limbs and 48 per cent by repairs. Two firms, Hanger and Vessa, supplied 70 per cent, by value, of all new limbs and a higher share of the repair market. Both firms are owned by the InterMed Group (a subsidiary of BTR plc) and the managing directors sit on each other's Boards. The Working Party found it difficult to believe, under these circumstances, that Hanger and Vessa could work independently from one another.

The Government is virtually a monopoly purchaser of limbs in the UK. Professor Michael Beenstock commented, when examining the structure of the industry, 'the broad picture that emerges was that of a monopsonist ... DHSS

---

[1] Royal College of Physicians, *Physical Disability in 1986 and Beyond*, London: RCP, 1986.

faced with 3 or 4 large sellers'. He went on to point out that:

> monopsony power could be exploited to drive very hard bargains with suppliers, but it seemed the converse had been true... [The] DHSS has abrogated its monopsony power and has transformed it into monopoly power in favour of the contractors.[1]

The limb companies have been profitable. For two out of the three years from 1980 to 1983 (the only years for which there was found to be complete data) limb manufacturers made profits, as a percentage of allowable costs, in excess of the DHSS target of 7.5 per cent. One firm, for example, had always achieved a maximum profit of 12.5 per cent and in the financial year 1980-81 retained profits of 14.5 per cent on costs, in recognition of efficiencies achieved.[2]

When considering the rates of return on capital employed Professor Beenstock reported that they were 'excessive by any standards and raised serious doubts as to whether the Government was indeed getting value for money'.[3] These returns which for 1981/82 ranged from 20% to 74%, were far in excess of the targeted returns ranging from 12% to 18% as indicated by the Review Board for Government Contracts in its fourth review. The shortcomings of the contractual situation which applied until 1985 were described in the Coopers & Lybrand Report at Appendix M of the McColl Report (Volume 2).

In sum, McColl finds present and past governments guilty of having failed to ensure that the artificial limb

---

[1] *Report,* Vol. 2, Annexe N, p. 1.

[2] *Op. cit.,* p. N3.

[3] *Ibid.*

service was run efficiently. The overall cost of the service was estimated to be about £38 million and yet there were

> no management accounts maintained which allow costs to be allocated to the different categories of patients or to the types of limbs supplied and no cost accounting exercise is undertaken.[1]

Client Satisfaction and Artificial Limbs

Research Surveys of Great Britain (RSGB) carried out a survey among artificial limb users in 1983.[2] A very high percentage (85 per cent) said that they were, on the whole, satisfied with their artificial limbs. However, over half the users questioned (52 per cent) also wanted some improvement made to their limbs. One of the improvements most frequently mentioned (by 23 per cent of amputees) was better fit and comfort. Many factors can be responsible for poorly fitting limbs including inappropriate amputation, inadequate prosthetic care and poor management. All three factors were found to have contributed to ineffectual fitting under the ALAC service.

The British Orthopaedic Association have confirmed that many amputations are performed by surgeons with insufficient experience;[3] and in a survey commissioned by the Working Party, 30 per cent were considered to have stump defects likely to prejudice seriously limb fitting.[4] Prosthetic

---

[1] Report, Vol. 1, para. 10.

[2] Research Surveys of Great Britain, A Survey Carried Out Among Artificial Limb Users, 1983. A summary of the main findings can be found in the Report, Vol. 2, Annexe G.

[3] British Orthopaedic Association, The Prosthetic and Orthotic Services in England and Wales and Northern Ireland, 1972.

[4] Report, Vol. 2, Annexe H.

care and practice is also blamed for ill-fitting limbs. Professor Radcliffe, a world authority on prosthetics, reported to the Working Party that:

> Not only do prosthetists in England often not know how to apply what is considered well-recognised principles of modern prosthetic technology, it is often difficult for them to accept instruction or criticism from abroad.[1]

Unfortunately the report on prosthetic training abroad, commissioned by the Working Party, was not published on the advice of DHSS lawyers. Nevertheless McColl followed it in his recommendation, that a degree in prosthetics and orthotics should be the normal requirement of practice.

Many of the complaints highlighted problems arising from failure to secure effective management. Late limb delivery was a major consumer complaint: of those users who had a limb supplied in the last five years, about one in six felt that the time taken for delivery was too long — the majority of these had waited two months or more.[2] An examination of the available data on delivery revealed that at least 50 per cent of all new limbs were being delivered late; and 40 per cent of major repairs and 25 per cent of general repairs were behind schedule. As McColl noted:

> delays are not just exasperating. They can of themselves cause further delay in rehabilitation, because stumps can and do change over time and a cast taken 6-8 weeks before delivery of the socket may well not fit at all so that the process has to start all over again.[3]

---

[1] *Report,* Vol. 1, para. 24.

[2] RSGB, *op. cit.*

[3] *Report,* Vol. 1, para. 34.

These delays, usually caused by outdated professional practices, did not occur in the other countries the working party visited. The limb companies were failing to meet the delivery times stipulated in their contracts and the DHSS had done very little about it. Indeed the contract times were considered by the Working Party to be too long, since the introduction of modular assembly from components should have speeded delivery.

As the limb companies have pointed out, delays were also caused by ALAC's appointment system and problems associated with the ambulance service. For example, a patient may arrive late at an ALAC and/or have to leave early in order to fit in with the ambulance's schedule. About two-thirds of all patients use ambulance transport and some face long journeys to their nearest centre. Ambulance services operate on a priority category basis and outpatient transport is not at the top of the list of priorities. The McColl Report pointed out that these arrangements needed to be improved.

Choice

One of the findings of the RSGB (1983) survey was that amputees were not being given enough say in their choice of limb. The main criticisms were lack of information, consultation and choice. Over fifty per cent of those interviewed said that their doctor had not discussed different types of artificial limb with them at all and very few amputees had been consulted about the limb firm (and hence the all-important prosthetist) to which they were allocated.

This lack of respect for the consumer is now acknowledged to be typical of public welfare services and is no longer surprising. However, it was also discovered that, in practice, choice was often not possible. Despite contractual arrangements imposed by the DHSS on limb companies to supply and repair each other's limbs, prosthetists attending

ALACs rarely prescribed limbs other than their company's own. In his present position the prosthetist is part salesman and part professional and his main allegiance is understandably to the limb company which employs him. In the 10 ALACs which contracted with only one limb firm this meant that, in practice, there was no choice for amputees. McColl recommended that every type of limb system supplied by the service should be available at every ALAC, irrespective of who employed the prosthetist working there.[1]

Value For Money

The Working Party seriously doubted whether the DHSS was getting value for money:

> There is no value for money assessment of the service provided by local contractors. In fact the present charging system obscures the cost message. It is not possible to relate the prices charged to the items supplied because average group prices apply. The reasons for this system are obscure but appear to stem from lack of DHSS staff resources and insufficient understanding of the possible consequences of the method. The only unit-based budgets are for expenditure on 'housekeeping' items. Bought in prosthetic costs are not identifiable to individual prosthetists, doctors or ALACs.[2]

McColl recommended splitting the limb-fitting contract into one for prosthetic services and another for hardware. This would, first, enable the true costs of the service to be identified and allow supplier prices for each element of service to be compared. Secondly, it would strengthen the advisory role of the prosthetist by enabling more impartial

---

[1] *Report,* Vol. 1, para. 38.

[2] *Op. cit.,* para. 33(c).

limb prescription; and thirdly, it would result in greater choice for patients.

Competition in the Supply of Artificial Limbs

Competition at all levels of the service was absent. The market share of each limb firm had not changed significantly for many years. InterMed, with a market share of over 70 per cent in lower limbs, enjoyed a monopoly through its subsidiaries. InterMed and Blatchford are the two major suppliers of conventional limbs, of the components from which to assemble modular limbs and of prosthetic services. Even where more than one contractor was represented at an ALAC, it was found that orders for new limbs were placed on the basis of 'Buggins' turn.[1]

The fact that manufacturing firms both employ and train prosthetists also made it difficult for new firms to enter the market. And the rigorous approval procedures applied to potential suppliers by the Government's Scientific and Technical Branch (STB), made it difficult for newcomers to compete with current suppliers. Otto Bock, a West German company, told the Monopolies and Mergers Commission (MMC) that for several years it did not submit its hardware components for testing because the company 'was not sure of the testing or the people who carried it out, or whether they would be influenced by the manufacturers'. They also agreed with the view that the English market was extremely difficult to enter because of the grip of the manufacturing companies which supplied prosthetic services.[2] The role of the STB was considered by the Working Party to have inhibited firms' product development and

---

[1] *Ibid.,* para. 51.

[2] The Monopolies and Mergers Commission, *Artificial Lower Limbs: A Report on the Supply of Artificial Limbs in the UK,* London: HMSO, April 1989, para. 3.36.

range of products available, restricting potential choice for patients even more. The justification for such rigorous testing procedures is not at all clear though the damage it has caused by reducing competition is evident; no new limb firms had entered the market for over 20 years.

The Wheelchair Service

Wheelchairs are provided by ALACs on receipt of a recommendation signed by either a GP or NHS hospital doctor. According to the extent of disability one of three types of chair may be prescribed: a non-powered wheelchair, a powered wheelchair for indoor use only or a powered outdoor chair which is attendant controlled. Occupant-controlled powered chairs for outdoor use are not available through ALACs. Once supplied, usually direct to the user, chairs are maintained by local approved repairers. Detailed information on wheelchair users is unfortunately not available. However it is known from DHSS data that there are approximately 400,000 wheelchair users in Britain. The majority of these are elderly people who use their wheelchair far less frequently than the 15 per cent who are totally reliant on their equipment for mobility. Many users in this latter group spend on average 64 hours a week in their chair.[1]

McColl defined the objective of the wheelchair service to be

to meet the basic need for short-range mobility of people of all ages who have serious and permanent difficulties in walking.[2]

---

[1] Office of Population Census and Surveys, *Wheelchairs and their Users*, DHSS, 1977 (Fenwick Report).

[2] *Report*, Vol. 1, para. 86.

And he identified three main problem areas in the wheel-chair service: assessment and prescription, hardware, and supply and repair. As with artificial limbs, these problems caused disabled people much unnecessary inconvenience and suffering.

Assessment and Prescription

Because of the lack of data the effectiveness of wheelchair prescriptions is unknown. However, the Association for Spina Bifida and Hydrocephalus has claimed that 90 per cent of young people with Spina Bifida who attend its clinics are in wheelchairs which are either unsuitable, need some adjustment or require further accessories. And the Disabled Living Research Unit, Mary Marlborough Lodge, informed the McColl Working Party that 50 per cent of the people that they see had inadequate wheelchairs 10 per cent of which are 'completely unsuitable or unsafe'.[1]

The problems caused by poor prescription and assessment are not usually serious for occasional users. However, for the seriously disabled they cause an unnecessary restriction in mobility often resulting not only in pain but deformity which may further reduce the individual's ability to live independently. The cause of these problems is the failure of prescribers to recommend the correct type of wheelchair user. The Fenwick Report (1977), for instance, noted that only 10 per cent of prescriptions involved a visit to an ALAC or NHS wheelchair clinic. McColl recommended improvements in the training of prescribers, particularly for those involved in complicated assessments. He advocated a two-tier prescribing and assessment procedure to reflect the two major categories of wheelchair users: the severely disabled who are totally reliant on their equipment and the

---

[1] *Op. cit.,* para. 88.

majority of users who are mainly elderly people who use their wheelchairs less than once a day.

Hardware

The range of wheelchairs supplied through ALAC was considered by the Working Party to be inadequate. Many elderly patients received equipment which was more sophisticated than required and many seriously disabled children and adults were being supplied with chairs which did not meet their needs. The Working Party recommended the introduction of a wheelchair designed for occasional use (low cost and low performance) mainly for the elderly and indoor/outdoor powered (occupant-controlled) and high performance wheelchairs for the more dependent. Inbucon Management Consultants estimated that the introduction of an occasional chair, assuming 70 per cent of users would be better suited to it than their current equipment, would give annual savings of up to £3.1 million.[1] The attendant-controlled powered chair, the only DHSS outdoor powered chair available, was described in the Report as 'grotesquely inadequate'.[2]

In view of these deficiencies it is not surprising that many disabled people buy their wheelchairs privately or have them bought for them by one of the charities. Recipients of Mobility Allowance also use their money to buy more suitable wheelchairs privately though they then have less to spend on long-range transport such as a car. The McColl Report blamed meanness on the part of government for these obvious gaps at the upper end of the DHSS wheel-chair range. The need of the disabled for personal indepen-dence cannot be satisfied while, as disabled spokesmen

---

[1] Inbucon Management Consultants, *Study of the Wheelchair Service Proposals Evaluation*, London: DHSS, 1985.

[2] *Report*, Vol. 1, para. 112.

point out, under the current provisions no disabled person can 'go out for a walk alone' and those without a companion are unable to go outside at all.[1]

Supply and Repair

The Working Party concluded that the 'ideal' arrangements for wheelchair supply would be for manufacturers to offer the equipment that they sell on the open market direct to ALAC patients subject to full product liability. The current set-up is far removed from this ideal. The DHSS lays down a wheelchair specification and awards contracts annually to suppliers after inviting competitive tenders. The majority of chairs on issue (approximately 80 per cent) are thus manufactured specifically for the ALAC service. Wheelchairs are not simply 'approved' by the government, as are artificial limbs; they are designed for it too. The justification for this practice is two-fold. First, standardisation is intended to facilitate the interchangeability of parts in order to reduce the cost of maintenance and repair. Hence the common practice of reconditioning chairs. Secondly, design specification is said to facilitate economies of scale and therefore lower prices. Inbucon's report to the Working Party, however, casts doubt upon the validity of these justifications,[2] arguing that it costs more to recondition wheelchairs centrally than to buy new ones, and that the potential savings from having standardised parts were, at the time of the Report, more than offset by their wasteful distribution (amounting to some £4.5 million).

Failure effectively to control the costs of wheelchair maintenance and repair was in extreme contrast to the keen tendering procedures adopted by the DHSS for new specifications. This combination of keen tendering and

---

[1] *Report*, Vol. 2, Annexe O.

[2] *Op. cit.*, Annexe P.

DHSS insistence on detailed specifications, coupled with the fact that the 'free' provision of wheelchairs severely curtails the private market for potential supply, has resulted in a loss-making industry, virtually closed to newcomers; the costs of tooling up to supply state wheelchairs are very unlikely to be recouped within common commercial time limits, at the prices offered by the Department. Detailed wheelchair specifications and low prices negotiated by civil servants have perpetuated traditional sources of supply. Despite the size of the state wheelchair market (the second largest in the world), wheelchair suppliers often choose to ignore it altogether and cater mainly for private paying customers.

The current process of supplying state wheelchairs has created a stagnant industry competing in an artificial domestic market. If it were not for the export market (all exported non-powered wheelchairs are proprietary designs) and the willingness of the disabled to raise private money to buy chairs, diversity and innovation in the British wheelchair industry would have been completely eliminated.[1] The Working Party duly recommended that:

> Central reconditioning of wheelchairs should stop... Performance specifications should replace design specification of existing DHSS wheelchairs... Contracts should be revised so that suppliers will be required in future to accept full product liability and to give an undertaking that they will manufacture special wheelchairs as necessary.[2]

These recommendations are not motivated by a desire for cost efficiency alone. Considering the diversity of needs amongst wheelchair users, it is of particular importance that

---

[1] *Report*, Vol. 2, Annexe N.

[2] *Report*, Vol. 1, para. 121.

state intervention does not stifle the innovative potential of competitive markets. Up to now this has indeed been the case and the changes recommended by McColl will go some way towards remedying the situation, but choice in wheelchairs will remain limited until wheelchair users are given personal purchasing power.

Vouchers

A key element of the McColl prescription for improving the ALAC service is the recommendation for:

> a cash option [which] should be introduced so that disabled people can change or enhance provision that is available through ALAC. This arrangement should allow those who wish to accept the available equipment to pay for non-essential extras which they require to satisfy personal preference or provide cash for those who want to buy their wheelchairs privately.[1]

Introducing a cash/voucher option into the ALAC service was discussed by the Working Party when they considered the supply of artificial limbs. However, it was felt that until prosthetic services were costed separately from hardware and prosthetists contracted to ALAC rather than suppliers, the introduction of vouchers would not be effective. Allowing amputees to top-up ALAC provision in order to get a different limb not normally supplied through the service was recommended. All the ALAC customers with whom the Working Party conferred supported a cash option as a means of achieving greater freedom of choice.

Under the current arrangements ALAC clients must either accept what the service has to offer or forgo help altogether. Only those disabled people with access to private

---

[1] *Op. cit.*, para. 106.

funds have the freedom to choose equipment that may best satisfy their needs and preferences. Choice in wheelchairs and artificial limbs does not necessarily imply the option, for some, to get 'better' equipment, though inequalities in provision to satisfy equal medically defined needs would undoubtedly occur, as at present. Wheelchairs, like shoes for the able-bodied, for example, come in different styles, materials, colours and designs. Individual requirements vary according to their personal preferences and lifestyle. Satisfactory wheelchair provision does not boil down to an accurate fulfilment of medically defined needs alone.

In view of the problems identified with the wheelchair industry a cash/voucher option would not only enhance choice for the disabled; it would also encourage suppliers to increase the quality and range of equipment manufactured. The creation of competition on the demand side, through the use of vouchers, would provide the incentive necessary for suppliers to become more dynamic and innovatory. Importantly, in this case, because the client group has a wide range of preferences, allowing the service user to become financially sovereign would encourage manufacturers to conduct market research to find out what their disabled customers want from their wheelchairs. Allowing the market a greater role in the future of the British wheelchair industry may produce equipment quite different from what the government would supply in order to satisfy the medical profession's definition of 'basic need'. The value of market provision is the incentive given to suppliers to produce what the paying customer requires. The Working Party's proposal for a cash/voucher option would convert the wheelchair user into the paying customer.

3

Implementing The McColl Report

Fortunately for disabled people the McColl Report was not destined to remain on the shelf, gathering dust, as some observers of government might have predicted. Just over a year after publication the Minister announced the Government's acceptance of the Report and their intention to reorganise ALAC services, and many of the changes recommended by McColl have already been implemented. However, at the expense of the disabled consumer, some of the Report's most progressive proposals including allowing ALAC users to top-up provision and the cash/voucher scheme for wheelchairs have been brushed aside. The disabled must still either accept the services ALAC offers, or forgo state help altogether.

Organisation and Management

In April 1986 Tony Newton, Minister for the Disabled, announced the first steps towards implementing the Report. The DHSS's disablement services had been brought together to form the Disablement Services Division, headed by a new general manager with responsibility for ALACs and for the medical, professional and technical staff serving them. The general manager is supported by a new director of operations and director of procurement brought in from the NHS.

In March 1987 the Government's intention to extend the principle of general management to the ALAC service at local level was announced. The ALAC service was to be reorganised into regions with boundaries co-terminous with the NHS. Each region would be headed by a regional general manager responsible for the entire limb and appliance service. The Minister also announced the setting up of a joint working party with the Orthotic and Prosthetic Training and Education Council (OPTEC), a government approved training body, to review the training of prosthetists. It was also officially accepted, as recommended by McColl, that the DHSS should no longer directly control ALACs. On 1 July 1987 an interim management board — the Disablement Services Authority (DSA) — in the form of a special health authority took over the running of ALAC services. The DSA is accountable directly to the Minister and comprises a Chairman, Lord Holderness, who is an amputee, Vice-Chairman, Professor Ian McColl and eight other members. The DSA has a threefold responsibility:

(a) to run the service until 31 March 1991.
(b) to build upon the improvements taking place in the service.
(c) to carry forward with regional health authorities the planning for the integration of the services with other health services on 1 April 1991.

The DSA was given its own budget for 1987-88 and planning figures for the two following years. According to the Minister special financial arrangements will also be made to safeguard funding for a period after integration with the NHS.[1] These interim management arrangements are illustrated in Table 1.

The new structure is intended to foster stronger links with the occupational therapy, physiotherapy and rehabilitation services provided by the NHS, and to strengthen management during the interim period. By September 1988, 14 DSA regions had been created, each headed by a regional manager based at the local Disablement Services Centre.

---

[1] DHSS, Press Release 87/104, March 1987.

Customer Services

Customer services have seen the most obvious improvements since the Report was published. ALACs have been renamed Disablement Services Centres (DSCs) and many have been physically improved and in some cases completely refurbished. The DSA is currently experimenting with new methods of making attendance at centres easier for patients. New transport and appointment systems have been introduced and since November 1987 a customer complaints procedure has been in operation. Access to clinics for patients living in outlying districts has been extended through the setting up of satellite centres and arrangements for dealing with cross-boundary flows. And all regional managers are reported to be making improvements to their local patient transport systems.[1]

Medical Services

The planned integration of the DSA into the NHS overtakes a number of the Report's proposals. The appointment of a clinical director at each ALAC is unlikely to be necessary since expertise in rehabilitation medicine will be provided by the NHS. ALAC medical officers are being given the opportunity to attend training courses designed to bring them up to the RCP required standard for accreditation in rehabilitation medicine. The problems caused by lack of co-ordination also have the potential to be resolved following integration with the NHS. However formal liaison arrangements may be necessary in, for example, the pre-operative assessment of amputees, if guaranteed improvements are to be made.

---

[1] DSA, *Introductory Guide*, October 1988.

Artificial Limbs

It is clear that the government accepted the need for changes in the artificial limb service before the Report was published.

Efficiency and Competition in Artificial Limb Supply

Following a comprehensive review of limb contracts the DHSS offered revised contracts to all contractors in December 1985. The major changes included a reduction in the target profit from 7.5 to 3.5 per cent on allowable costs and the inclusion of a clause seeking damages for late limb deliveries. Immediately the managing director of Hanger made a fierce and public protest against cutting agreed profit limits. Hanger and Vessa insisted that their contracts could not be changed in the manner proposed and instituted legal proceedings against the DHSS aimed at securing a declaratory injunction that the 1985 contracts should continue for three further years. The DHSS and subsequently the DSA defended the actions. Judgement in both was declared in the DSA's favour in December 1987. In the interim, however, patient services were severely disrupted. InterMed withdrew certain services twice in 1986 because it wanted price increases, and some conventional limb types were again withdrawn in 1987. The supply was resumed after the DSA conceded price increases. At the same time Hanger reorganised its manufacturing activity which resulted in a strike and dispute lasting to June 1987 which further disrupted supplies to patients.

Commentators from outside the Department believe that the civil service could have handled the situation better. Even so, it is clear that the necessary concern of the public sector to provide an uninterrupted artificial limb service weakened the DHSS/DSA's bargaining power. It enabled InterMed to exert an undesirable amount of pressure on the public purchasing bodies. The MMC rightly considered the actions of InterMed to have had effects adverse to the public interest.[1] It recommends that in order to increase competition and prevent future disruptions

> InterMed should be divided; this should take the form of InterMed Ltd and its ultimate holding company divesting themselves of ownership and control of the reference goods either of J E Hanger & Co Ltd or Vessa Ltd within six months beginning on 30 April 1989. Neither company should be sold to the other monopolist, Chas A Blatchford & Sons Ltd. If InterMed chooses to divest itself of both companies, such divestment should not be to the same owner.[2]

The commission also recommended that InterMed be required to supply lower limbs to any public sector purchaser or contractor on the same terms, conditions and prices as they were made available to its own prosthetists; and that the DSA submit a further report on the progress towards a more competitive market by the end of September 1990.

Since its establishment the DSA has sought to introduce more satisfactory contractual arrangements. This is a crucial element of its overall policy for improving services. It is currently in the process of contracting separately for the provision of prosthetic services and hardware supply (as recommended by McColl), and has replaced the cost-based form of contract, which had existed for 40 years, with competitively tendered contracts.

The results of the latest round of tendering for prosthetic services at DSCs are imminent. Prosthetists have been actively encouraged by the DSA to set up companies and bid for the contracts. Ex-Hanger prosthetists who have formed the company Rehabilitation Services Limited,

---

[1] MMC, *op. cit.*, para. 8.28.

[2] *Ibid.*, para. 8.33(a).

successfully bid for the contract to service North East Thames Region. At present there are only a few firms of independent prosthetists contracted to the DSA but it is likely that more will win contracts in the future. The initiative at North East Thames has already resulted in improvements in limb delivery times. Agreement has also now been reached with the limb contractors to ensure that all limb systems will be supplied to all DSCs regardless of who employs the prosthetist working there, and for improved delivery times in all regions.

The new contracts also require limb manufacturers to use British Standards quality assurance schemes which should enable a reduction in the role of the Scientific and Technical Branch (STB) in artificial limb production. The current system, which requires limb components to pass a series of tests before they can be made available on prescription, could be dispensed with. Shifting away from centralised liability for safety standards and control towards manufacturers' product liability will make British equipment more competitive in world markets and increase the range of products available to amputees. There is no comparable approval system in Scotland and Wales. They follow the advice resulting from the English tests but are not limited by it. Thus, limb-fitting centres outside England have been more readily able to introduce European limb systems.

Choice

Competition and choice in the supply of artificial limbs has recently been enhanced by the introduction into ALAC of a major European limb system supplied by the West German company, Otto Bock. Unfortunately, the supply of these limbs is severely limited by the number of British prosthetists able to fit them.

Prosthetic Training

The inadequacies of British prosthetic training highlighted in the Report, have been accepted by the DSA, and the future of the profession is currently under discussion. A degree in prosthetics and orthotics is likely to become the required qualification for practice. Strathclyde University, which offers such a degree course, is increasing its yearly student intake and plans to offer up-grading courses to established practitioners. It is envisaged that a degree course will also be offered by the University of Salford. However, a shorter more basic qualification equivalent to an HND, will have to be retained not least to help overcome the shortage of practitioners which will be made worse once the degree courses get under way.

Wheelchairs

Recent Initiatives

In early 1987, the Minister for the Disabled announced several initiatives, recommended by the Working Party, to improve the wheelchair service including development of a new chair specially designed for the needs of children and a low cost chair for occasional users. The latter initiative has yet to materialise despite the likely advantages it would bring to both user and funder (and Inbucon estimated that as many as 70 per cent of current wheelchair users would be more suited to an occasional chair).[1] He also announced the extension of the service to include responsibility for supply of special seating support (a type of orthosis) for wheelchair users. At present there is complete separation in the provision of wheelchairs and orthoses which are supplied through the NHS. This organisational anomaly

---

[1] *Report,* Vol. 2, Annexe T.

creates difficulties for patients and practitioners. For example, when a moulded type chair or matrix chair is required the seat or mould is made by an orthotist and funded by the NHS the wheelchair is, however, provided by the DSA. This arrangement often leads to unnecessary and lengthy delays in the provision of the finished product. The integration of ALAC into the NHS should help overcome the problems of service co-ordination but is unlikely, alone, to solve the many other problems experienced by users of the orthotic service (discussed in Chapter 4).

Indoor/Outdoor Powered Wheelchairs

The introduction of indoor/outdoor occupant controlled powered wheelchairs is presently being considered by the DSA. At the beginning of this year a pilot study was initiated to supply such chairs to selected clients in two NHS regions. The outcome of this trial is likely to determine the future of indoor/outdoor wheelchair provision. Meanwhile, the DSA does not officially provide this type of chair. As discussed earlier this is a serious gap in the wheelchair service, incompatible with the general objective of 'meeting the basic need for short-range mobility' of the disabled as defined by McColl and with the Government's aim of enabling disabled people to live as independent a life as possible.

Prescription and Assessment

More encouragingly, steps are being taken to improve wheelchair assessment and prescription. Talks are underway with the therapy professions to improve training and the wheelchair prescription form has been redesigned to ensure a qualified therapist is consulted. Indeed it is envisaged that GPs will no longer be the principal prescribers of wheelchairs. District health services are also preparing to increase their involvement in wheelchair assessment and prescription and three regional wheelchair clinics have recently been opened.

Maintenance and Repair

The inefficient practice of centrally reconditioning wheelchairs is planned to stop completely before 1991 and new local reconditioning contracts were started in April 1988. Also, the end of free-issue spares to wheelchair repairers has been agreed in principle and competitive tendering for repair services to a region on a fixed-cost basis is underway.

A New Improved ALAC?

Although there have been some improvements to the wheelchair service, they should not distract attention from the obstacles that remain to the creation of a competitive and hence innovative wheelchair industry. Manufacturers are still working to government design specifications for ALAC-supplied chairs, and consumers are still unable to enhance or change any ALAC equipment. The STB continues to 'approve' artificial limbs and to be involved in the detail of wheelchair manufacture. This is despite the fact that most manufacturers supplying the DSA are already approved by the Good Manufacturing Practice Scheme of the NHS procurement directorate (which means that those manufacturers have achieved the quality required by the British Standards Institution).

In the short life of the DSA much has been achieved but much more remains to be done if the benefits of a competitive market are to be realised. One of the Report's most far-reaching recommendations, the cash/voucher proposal, has been rejected and others have been implemented in half measure only. For example, requiring prosthetists to bid for a service contract is a step in the right direction, but only if the best firm wins. The 'best' cannot be equated with the cheapest where quality of service is of equal importance. McColl urged that prosthetic services should be monitored and failure to implement this recommendation will significantly dilute the benefit of his proposals.

4

NHS Services for the Disabled: the Orthotic Service

Privatisation

The McColl recommendations go beyond a call for more competition in the supply of ALAC services. If privatisation can be taken to mean the rolling back of the activities of the state, then in sum the McColl prescription adds up to a privatisation proposal. However, from the outset ALAC services, though publicly funded, have always been supplied through a public/private mix. In examining the McColl proposals we are therefore attempting to evaluate the merit of tipping the balance in favour of private provision. Indeed, service users should have the option of rejecting the state equipment on offer, taking the monetary equivalent instead (in cash or voucher form) and buying equipment of their choice on the open market.

By arguing in favour of a competitive market and a reduction in the role of the state in the supply of ALAC services, we have added flesh to the assertion that the private market may be a superior mechanism for distributing many welfare goods and services usually provided by state bureaucracies. Can we thus be accused of the 'philistine resurrection of economic man'?[1] Has the least-cost notion of efficiency been our primary concern? We think not. The aim of this discussion has been to inform the debate on services for the disabled of the likely impact of a competitive market on the efficiency and quality of services. On both criteria we are led to recommend a change in the

---

[1]   Titmuss, R.M., *The Gift Relationship*, London: Allen & Unwin, 1970, p. 14.

balance of ALAC provision towards a competitive market. The introduction of a cash/voucher option and allowing users to top-up ALAC equipment with private funds would be firm steps towards furthering this aim.

Supporters of state provision (as distinct from state finance), in particular, are unlikely to agree with our conclusions. First, critics of privatisation might argue that greater state involvement in service provision than we propose is necessary to check the potential for exploitation of service users by suppliers seeking to maximise profits rather than meet needs. As far as services for the disabled are concerned, clients may be in a particularly weak position to evaluate the claims of private providers. Critics point out that not even better public regulation of private suppliers will be sufficient to ensure that they operate in the interests of those they are supposed to serve. Secondly, it is argued that private markets are undesirable in welfare provision because they are likely to widen inequalities in the distribution of services.

In response to the first charge, it is a major merit of vouchers that they would create increased demand for more accurate, comparable information on private suppliers than does the present system of monopoly provision through the DSCs. Such information would enable service users to determine how best to provide for themselves, within the limits of the medical prescription, thereby encouraging independence and enhancing consumer satisfaction. It is the proper role of government to regulate information on welfare goods and services supplied through a competitive private market. Manufacturers' advertisements, for example, could be required to give information about the qualities of wheelchairs in a common format so as to facilitate comparisons between chairs. Finally, the introduction of competition through the provision of a cash/voucher option would force manufacturers to find out the needs of consumers and be more eager to determine the degree to which their products

succeed in meeting them. For those disabled people who
have no wish to shop in the open market for equipment or
who are unable to do so, the DSC would provide. It should
be remembered that McColl proposed a cash/voucher
option.

The second likely charge against private provision makes
the common mistake of assuming that one of the purposes
of state welfare provision has been the creation of equality.
Historically, the welfare state was not developed on the
basis of egalitarian principles, but rather to extend the rights
of democratic citizenship.[1] As such it merely intends to
guarantee certain minimum rights to welfare services. In
wheelchairs this can be interpreted as the right to the
means to fulfil 'the basic need for short-range mobility of
people of all ages who have serious and permanent
difficulties walking.'[2] Within that remit the McColl Report is
a solution to the ills of ALAC. The support it gives to a
competitive market comprising numerous sellers and buyers
is founded on the well-recognised ability of markets to
produce, over time, rising standards of service to meet
'basic needs'.

NHS Disablement Services

The McColl Working Party was quite clear in its view that
ALAC services should remain outside the NHS:

> We believe that it is imperative not only to maintain a
> separate management control...but also to fund the
> services separately as at present.[3]

---

[1] Marshall, T.H., *Sociology at the Crossroads*, London: Heinemann, 1963.

[2] *Report,* Vol. 1, para. 86.

[3] *Ibid.,* para. 148.

Separate management control was thought necessary because it was unrealistic to expect that the RHAs could implement separately the changes recommended. It is now accepted that by 1991 the ALAC service should have sufficient management direction to be devolved to regions, which would facilitate co-ordination with local NHS disability services.

There is, unfortunately, no detailed data on the disability services currently being provided by the NHS. What information is available, however, suggests that the Working Party was right to be concerned about handing over ALAC to the NHS. The RCP reported considerable unevenness of provision between different regions and districts; and widespread lack of co-ordination between services resulting in omissions and duplication of services, delays in obtaining help and discontinuity of help as the patient is referred from one service to another. A frequent complaint is the inadequate information given to disabled patients about the nature of their condition, proposed treatment, opportunities and services available.[1] Such deficiencies suggest that the NHS needs to put its disablement services in order before incorporating ALAC. There is also the danger that standards of ALAC provision will diminish because, once established in the NHS, ALAC services will have to compete for monies with higher-profile medical specialties. Three areas are currently given priority in service funding by the NHS: mental illness, mental handicap and care of the elderly. We agree with the RCP (1986) that physical disability should become a fourth such area.

---

[1] RCP, *op. cit.*

Orthotics

The orthotic service, organised through the NHS, was not included in the remit of the McColl Working Party. However, references made to the service during the McColl investigations led the Working Party to believe the service to be in a parlous state. This view has been recently confirmed by the findings of a report by the NHS Management Consultancy Services.[1]

There is no centrally collated data on the volume and costs of the orthotic service, although it is estimated in the NHS Management Consultancy Services report that the provision of appliances costs the NHS in excess of £40 million per annum. The most common orthotic devices issued are special footwear, but the range of appliances is wide and includes spinal supports, lower limb splints and abdominal appliances (eg trusses). Less commonly prescribed orthoses include elastic stockings, collars, artificial breasts and wigs. The vast majority of appliances are supplied by commercial companies and fitted by their own orthotists who attend clinical sessions in NHS hospitals. There are also a number of NHS employed orthotists (approximately 30) and some 13 NHS workshops, a few providing specialist service for the provision of the more complex appliances.

In many patients the need for an orthotic device is usually permanent. Further, patients may require several orthoses during their lifetime. Brace treatment of scoliosis is a good example. The affected patients are growing and the orthosis has to be replaced at regular intervals. Depending on its type, a spinal orthosis can cost anything from £225 to £350 and if the patient requires four or five such orthoses during their period of growth, the cost of treatment

---

[1] *Study of the Orthotic Service*, London: NHS Management Consultancy Services, 1988.

incurred by the NHS for orthotic equipment alone is substantial. Other orthoses are more expensive. A pair of cosmetic calipers costs over £300, a swivel walker and standing frame each over £500, and a reciprocating gait orthosis over £1,500.

In 1985 responsibility for negotiating the national contract for the supply of orthoses to all health authorities passed from the DHSS to North West Thames Regional Health Authority (NWTRHA). The 'contract' specifies required manufacturing standards, maximum delivery times and charges but does not confer on the participants a commitment to purchase and supply. It is really a method of arriving at an agreed price list which is distributed to the rest of the NHS. In 1986 the national contract was estimated to be worth some £40 million to the orthotic industry and embraced 137 contractors, and over 1,300 items.

Local Districts call for tenders on the basis of how much firms will be willing to discount the NWTRHA price list. This fiercely price-competitive tendering process is argued to have resulted in the elimination of smaller companies, which would be acceptable in the pursuit of efficiency if it were not for the widely held belief that economies are being achieved at the expense of quality and the long-term future of the industry. The NHS study team commented that:

> whilst this development does achieve short-term savings in the total cost of the service, if a supplier is chosen without reference to considerations other than cost, or the interests of other professions, the overall value of any savings achieved must be in doubt. Apart from the lack of regard for quality, there must be long-term misgivings about the cost consequences which will result from the reduction in the number of suppliers.[1]

---

[1] *Ibid.,* para. 3.3.7.

Just as with wheelchairs and artificial limbs, there is also dissatisfaction with the process for assessing new orthoses. Before a new appliance can be made available on prescription it is first assessed by a panel which includes representatives from the DHSS and NWTRHA. It is believed by professionals and manufacturers that this body may not have sufficient expertise to examine all new equipment presented to them. Furthermore, the procedures involved in the acceptance of a new item are argued to be cumbersome. One source in the industry told us that a new and improved brace for paraplegics had been developed in Britain. Yet, despite the size of the NHS market, this item is being marketed in the US and not the UK because of the difficulty of getting it accepted for issue by the NHS.

We recommend that responsibility for assessing the suitability of new orthoses, prostheses and wheelchairs for inclusion in national supply contracts be passed to a new research management board. This new board should comprise in the main clinicians and therapists with experience and expertise in prosthetics, orthotics and wheelchairs.

Other commonly expressed dissatisfactions with the orthotic service include:

Hardware. Many orthoses on issue are old-fashioned, ugly and badly-fitting.

Supply. The supply of orthoses is often slow and erratic, particularly when the device has to be specially made.

Access. There is unevenness in provision between different regions and districts. Due to the problems in charging for cross-boundary flows, patients suffer excessive delays in treatment and run the risk of outright denial. When the NHS fails to provide funds charities often step in, but this is clearly not a satisfactory basis for providing a national service.

Co-ordination. Responsibility for the care of patients is badly co-ordinated which results in fragmented treatment, service omissions and delays.

Choice. Most health authorities deal with only one, possibly two, orthotic firms and rely on the orthotist employed by the firm for advice on the most suitable equipment. The orthotist will usually supply his own firm's product. Effectively there is no choice in hardware or orthotist for patients unless private funds can be found.

Research. Under present arrangements there is no incentive for firms to engage in research and development. Hence the criticism that British orthoses are notoriously outdated.

Orthotists. During the McColl investigations into the training of limb-fitters it became apparent that the training of orthotists was also grossly inadequate.

At the end of this paper we make some proposals designed to deal with the worst of these failings.

5

Lessons From America

Provision of Limbs, Appliances and Wheelchairs under Medicare

Medicare is a Federal health insurance scheme run by the Health Care Financing Administration of the US Department of Health and Human Services. Medicare pays for wheelchairs and prosthetic and orthotic devices for people with disabilities under 65 years who have been entitled to social security disability payments for at least two years and all people aged 65 years and older. Provided the disabled person has a valid medical prescription signed by a doctor and has paid the yearly deductible (the first $75 of covered expenses in 1988) Medicare will pay 80 per cent of the 'approved charges' for the equipment supplied. The renting of equipment, which is far more common in America than in Britain, is organised along similar lines.

Orthotic and prosthetic devices and wheelchairs are supplied by medical equipment retailers. The equipment is fitted by therapists who usually work on the retailers' premises. Medicare makes one payment to the retailer which covers the cost of the equipment supplied and the therapist's services. The Medicare Administration is not concerned with the contractual relationships between retailer, therapist and manufacturer. Private insurance organisations called carriers are contracted by the Federal Government to make the Medicare payments.

The Medicare Administration does not commission equipment for beneficiaries. In stark contrast to Britain all equipment supplied by Medicare is bought or hired on the open market. And as might be expected the type and range of equipment available from retailers is vast.

Medicare Payments

Medicare payments for equipment and services supplied to beneficiaries are based on amounts approved by the Medicare carrier. The approved charge for each item or service will be either the customary charge (the charge most frequently made by the supplier for that item or service) or the prevailing charge based on all the customary charges in the locality, whichever is the lowest. Beneficiaries are free to top-up the Medicare payment if they wish to have more expensive equipment.

Maintenance and Repair

Suppliers bill the Medicare carrier for the cost of replacing and repairing equipment. Up to 10 per cent of the purchase price of a wheelchair is available for repairs but there is no renewal policy: once supplied wheelchairs are replaced only if there is an overwhelming medical requirement to do so. Artificial limbs are repaired and replaced under Medicare according to medical need. Wheelchairs are not reconditioned. Permanently disabled people always receive new equipment, and the temporarily immobile are likely to be given rented chairs. The decision to rent or buy is the beneficiary's. However, the Medicare carrier which handles claims in an area is required to review all claims for wheelchairs and, if the cost of renting is lower than buying, only the rental payments will be met by Medicare.

Lessons

The most obvious benefit of the American system is the high quality and wide variety of equipment and limbs available to Medicare beneficiaries. And because of the incentives created by competitive markets continually to improve upon existing standards, the level of provision in the USA has risen steadily.

The American service is, however, experiencing two significant problems. First, it is felt by the Medicare Administration that beneficiaries do not shop around for equipment sufficiently. One explanation is that third-party funding has created a moral hazard because in the past both consumers and providers faced weak incentives to contain costs. The introduction of an approved scale of charges as a payment base and co-insurance (part-payment by the customer) are expected to increase financial responsibility and encourage shopping around in the future. The bundling together of hardware and therapists' costs under Medicare also makes shopping around difficult in practice. The provision of wheelchairs, appliances and artificial limbs involves two separate sets of decisions on the part of the consumer, one set relating to the therapist, the other to the hardware. In order to maximise choice and competition these two elements should be recognised as separate, as recommended by McColl.

A second cause of concern to the Medicare Administration is the inadequacy of the medical prescription. As in Britain, it is believed that equipment is often either over- or under-prescribed. It is hoped in America to introduce Peer Review Organisations into the scheme to encourage professionals to improve their prescribing practice. Britain, as McColl stressed, should also routinely monitor the adequacy of prescriptions.

The experience of America also gives us some clues about how to determine the value of a state voucher/cash allowance with which disabled people would be expected to purchase equipment. As has already happened in the provision of ALAC wheelchairs, the tendency might be for the NHS to abuse its monopsony power and make the value of the voucher too low, thus perpetuating the current stagnation of the industries. On the other hand, governments cannot provide the equivalent of the Rolls-Royce wheelchair to all who want it. The use of approved charges in America is believed to have the potential accurately to reflect the market price of the equipment prescribed. And approved charges for wheelchairs have been successful in determining a value which is sufficient (a) to meet the medical prescription; (b) to be acceptable to government; and (c) to allow manufacturers a return sufficient for research and product development to be carried out. These three criteria should guide the value of a British voucher.

6

Conclusions and Proposals

The findings of the McColl Report are evidence that governments should not attempt both to finance and to control the production of health-care services. The disadvantages of doing so through ALAC have been borne by the disabled. And it is these people, one of the poorest groups in our society and therefore the least likely to be able to escape state provision and go private, who have been forced to suffer the bad service that absence of competition encourages.

The American Medicare programme does not offer us a ready-made alternative, but it does illustrate the benefits of a system combining state finance with competitive private provision. The quality and variety of equipment easily available in the US gives us a benchmark with which to compare the British service. The new ALAC service under the DSA promises to extend the competition and choice already brought into the service. But, until vouchers or grants are made available, what we shall be seeing is merely competition between sub-contractors who wish to supply DSCs and the NHS. This will be of help in obtaining value for money, but it will not be competition based on the availability of alternatives to paying consumers. Consequently it will not produce the supply-side effects that we might expect if consumers were made sovereign.

ALAC stands as a warning to enthusiasts for state provision (as distinct from state finance) and suggests to us that, wherever possible, consumers themselves should be given purchasing power.

Summary of Proposals

- Physical disability services should be given priority in funding by the NHS, as suggested in the RCP Report (1986).

- An optional voucher scheme should be introduced so that disabled people can *change* or *enhance* equipment supplied through DSCs and the NHS (including wheelchairs, artificial limbs and orthoses). The value of the voucher must reflect the market price of the equipment required to fulfil the medical prescription, and must be sufficient to cover the costs of equipment maintenance and repair.

- Professionals involved in the care of the disabled including prosthetists, orthotists and wheelchair therapists should be subject to performance audit along the lines of medical audit.

- The appointments and related patient transport systems must continue to be improved.

- All disabled patients must be made aware early in their rehabilitation of the choices available to them, subject to medical prescription.

- Contracts for wheelchairs, limbs and orthoses supplied through DSCs and the NHS should ensure that individual prices for all items prescribed can be identified.

- Equipment supplied by the NHS and DSCs should be approved under the relevant British Standard. The present role of the STB in approving equipment could then be dispensed with. Independent experts, accountable to a new Research Management Board, could be hired to carry out quality assurance inspections of manufacturers.

■ A Research Management Board should be established to evaluate new wheelchairs, artificial limbs and appliances, and decide whether or not they should be introduced into the NHS and DSCs either nationally or on a trial basis at a specialised unit. The Board should include members who are fully aware of the clinical and technical problems associated with the more complex wheelchairs, prostheses and orthoses.

■ The DSA should charge contractors for space at DSCs. The charging of such a 'market' rent would exercise a useful discipline on both the DSC management and the suppliers encouraging them to be more efficient.

■ Arrangements to integrate the training of prosthetists and orthotists should proceed as quickly as possible. Following the completion of training the individual should be able to work as an accredited orthotist, prosthetist or both.

■ The integrated training of prosthetists and orthotists to degree level at Salford University should be instituted as soon as possible. At the same time, the number of trainees at Strathclyde University should be increased.

■ Courses in orthotics and prosthetics should have easy access to a centre of excellence in the treatment of physical disability. And training should be given in an institution with a strong para-medical orientation so that the student orthotist/prosthetist can develop good working relationships with physiotherapists and occupational therapists during training.

■ Firms of individual prosthetists should be contracted to provide services at *all* relevant DSCs. Other therapists too should be encouraged to set up business independently.

■ Performance specifications should replace design specifications of wheelchairs supplied through DSCs and the NHS. Independent experts could be hired to draw up such specifications.

■ Wheelchairs should be leased under a rent-and-repair agreement from private suppliers or even other DSCs if it would be more economical than buying. A voucher could be given to patients who wish to make their own rental arrangements.

■ 'High performance' and dual-purpose powered wheelchairs (or the monetary equivalent) should be routinely provided for disabled people in receipt of a medical prescription.

■ A medical equipment amnesty should be declared in all NHS districts to encourage the return of wheelchairs and appliances (eg walking frames) no longer in use. DSCs should then be given the power to charge patients for equipment not returned.

Glossary

ALAC Artificial Limb and Appliance Centre (see also DSC — in 1987 ALACs were renamed DSCs).

Contractor A company which is under contract to supply and maintain artificial limbs to a public purchasing authority.

DHSS Department of Health and Social Security.

DSA Disablement Services Authority.

DSC Disablement Services Centre (formerly known as ALAC).

Dual-purpose powered chair A powered wheelchair that can be used both indoors and outdoors.

GP General Practitioner.

Modular limb An artificial limb, the greater part of which can be assembled on the spot from adaptable prefabricated components.

MMC Monopolies and Mergers Commission.

NHS National Health Service.

NWTRHA North West Thames Regional Health Authority.

OPTEC Orthotic and Prosthetic Training and Education Council.

Orthosis A device or external appliance to promote limb function (excluding prostheses).

Orthotic Denotes orthopaedic appliances other than artificial limbs.

Orthotist A person practising orthotics.

Prosthesis A surgical prosthesis is an artefact replacing a bodily deficiency. The prosthesis may be external (eg artificial limb) or internal (eg replacement of part or the whole of a bone or joint).

Prosthetic Concerned with prostheses.

Prosthetist A person concerned with limb-fitting.

RCP Royal College of Physicians.

RSGB Research Surveys of Great Britain Ltd.

STB Scientific and Technical Branch.

IEA Health Unit

Why not take out a Subscription?

To ensure receipt of all IEA Health Unit publications fill in this form and return it to:

> The Director,
> IEA Health Unit,
> 2 Lord North Street,
> London SW1P 3LB

I would like to subscribe beginning ....

☐ As an **Individual Subscriber** (paying personally) I enclose a Cheque/P.O. for £7.50.

☐ As a **Corporate Subscriber** I enclose a Cheque/P.O. for not less than £25. This will enable me to receive all publications plus periodic reports on the Unit's work.

Please charge £ .... to my credit card account Access / Visa / American Express / Diner's Club (Please delete as appropriate).

Account number ....

I would like to offer additional support for the IEA Health Unit's educational work and enclose a donation of £ ....

Name ....

Institution ....

Address ....

....

....

> **or**
> **Telephone**
> **01-799 3745**
> *With your Credit Card details*

HUP7

IEA Health Unit

The IEA Health Unit was founded towards the end of 1986 by the Institute of Economic Affairs to carry out scholarly studies of the NHS and the alternative mixed public/private systems of health care which predominate overseas. It has two particular objectives. First, it investigates how to enhance individual choice by promoting greater competition in the supply of health-care services. Second, it examines alternative methods of ensuring that no one goes in want of essential medical care due to their inability to pay.

SPECIAL OFFER

Acceptable Inequalities? *Essays on the Pursuit of Equality in Health Care*, April 1988.

RUDOLF KLEIN, Professor of Social Policy, University of Bath.
ROBERT PINKER, Professor of Social Work Studies, London School of Economics.
PETER COLLISON, Professor of Social Studies, University of Newcastle upon Tyne.
A. J. CULYER, Professor of Economics, University of York.

NOW AVAILABLE FOR LESS THAN HALF PRICE
Normally priced £8·95, it is now available for £4·00 (post free).

SOME EARLY REVIEWS ...
Rudolf Klein, in distinguishing between acceptable differences and unacceptable inequalities delivers some blows at the Black Report which dent it even if they do not demolish it ...

A. J. Culyer ... suggests that most egalitarians in health policy are closet 'national health' maximisers, whose real belief is that greater resource equality will actually promote better health and what they should realise is that they really favour his input-output approach to policy. *Health Services Management*

To begin with, take the pamphlet's title, *Acceptable Inequalities?*. Well, even allowing for the question mark, that is a breeze of fresh air for a start. But read on. According to the authors, 'You can have too much equality'. *The Times*

- -

ORDER FORM

Please supply me with .... copy/copies of **Acceptable Inequalities?**.

Price £4·00 each, post free. I enclose a cheque for ....
Invoice required: Yes/No.

Name ....

Company/Organisation ....

Address ....

....

....

Press Reactions to Other Health Unit Publications

Medicines in the Marketplace

June 1987, £5.95

DAVID G. GREEN, *Director, IEA Health Unit*

'If David Green's paper, the first in a series to be published by this unit, is anything to go by, a series of fascinating debates is due to follow . . . Dr Green packs in a wealth of information to support his clearly stated argument, which makes what could be a boring subject into a really good read.'
Nursing Standard

'Green's criticisms have some merit.' *British Medical Journal*

Efficiency and the NHS: A Case for Internal Markets?

February 1988, £4.50

RAY ROBINSON, *Kings Fund Institute*

'. . . the best critique so far of the internal market.'
The Independent, Guide to the NHS Debate

'An internal market would take the power of decision-making about treatment even further away from patients. "It would be district general managers who would make block decisions about where patients should be treated", Mr Robinson says.' *The Times*

Acceptable Inequalities? Essays on the Pursuit of Equality in Health Care

April 1988, £4.00

RUDOLF KLEIN, *Professor of Social Policy, University of Bath*

ROBERT PINKER, *Professor of Social Work Studies, London School of Economics*

PETER COLLISON, *Professor of Social Studies, University of Newcastle upon Tyne*

A. J. CULYER, *Professor of Economics, University of York*

'An interesting and provocative book . . .' *British Medical Journal*

'. . . stimulating reading and will help ensure that this particular debate remains high on the health agenda.' *Health Education Journal*

Keeping the Lid on Costs? Essays on Private Health Insurance and Cost-Containment in Britain

September 1988, £5.95

WILLIAM LAING, *Senior Partner, Laing and Buisson*

ROY FORMAN, *Managing Director, PPP*

NANCY SALDANA, *Head of Hospital Negotiations, PPP*

BRIAN BRICKNELL, *Personal Membership Director, BUPA*

'This short book sets a new standard of frankness about the problems of the private sector, not just in controlling costs but in maintaining quality of care ... This IEA health unit paper is a useful contribution.'
Nicholas Bosanquet, *The Health Service Journal*

American Health Care: What Are the Lessons for Britain?

January 1989, £5.95

CLARK C. HAVIGHURST, *Professor of Law, Duke University*

ROBERT B. HELMS, *Assistant Secretary, Department of Health and Human Services, Washington*

CHRISTOPHER BLADEN, *Department of Health and Human Services*

MARK PAULY, *Professor of Economics, University of Pennsylvania*

'A report ... from the Institute of Economic Affairs health unit, an influential think tank ... which attacks the "restrictive practices" operated by the medical establishment...' *Sunday Times*

'Restrictive practices enjoyed by doctors should be scrapped ... a report from the Institute of Economic Affairs says today.'
Daily Telegraph

Should Doctors Advertise?

March 1989, £3.00

David G. Green, *Director, IEA Health Unit*

'The General Medical Council should be stripped of its power to interfere with doctors' advertising because it obstructs competition, said Dr David Green, *British Medical Journal*

'Despite claims that [professional] disciplinary codes protect the public, they are seen to serve the interests of bad and indifferent doctors by David Green, *Health Service Journal*

WITHDRAWN

3005264510